REVISED EDITION

LADO PICTURE DICTIONARY

INTERMEDIATE WORKBOOK

Robert Lado

Contributing Writers
John Chapman
Barbara Barysh

Prentice Hall Regents, Upper Saddle River, NJ 07458

Publisher: **Mary Jane Peluso**
Production Editors/Pagers: **Jan Sivertsen/Steven Greydanus/Paula Williams/Kelly Tavares**
Manufacturing Manager: **Ray Keating**
Electronic Art Production and Scanning: **Todd Ware, Marita Froimson**
Art Director: **Merle Krumper**

Illustrated by Len Shalansky

In Memory of
Dr. Robert Lado

PRENTICE HALL REGENTS
A VIACOM COMPANY

©1996 by PRENTICE HALL REGENTS
Prentice-Hall, Inc.
A Simon & Schuster Company
Upper Saddle River, New Jersey 07458

Printed in the United States of America
10 9 8 7 6 5 4 3 2 1

ISBN 0-13-521519-6

Prentice-Hall International (UK) Limited, *London*
Prentice-Hall of Australia Pty. Limited, *Sydney*
Prentice-Hall Canada Inc., *Toronto*
Prentice-Hall Hispanoamericana, S.A., *Mexico*
Prentice-Hall of India Private Limited, *New Delhi*
Prentice-Hall of Japan, Inc., *Tokyo*
Simon & Schuster Asia Pte. Ltd., *Singapore*
Editora Prentice-Hall do Brasil, Ltda., *Rio de Janeiro*

CONTENTS

TO THE TEACHER

The **Intermediate Workbook,** which accompanies the *Lado Picture Dictionary*, Revised Edition, provides vocabulary practice for intermediate-level ESL/EFL students. Lessons are presented in the same order as the *Dictionary* material, and each workbook page provides a skills practice utilizing the specific vocabulary listed on each *Dictionary* page. The unit titles and lessons, along with the corresponding *Dictionary* pages, are listed in the **Workbook**. All instruction lines are short and simple, and the first answer in each exercise is always supplied. A unit vocabulary review and a personal writing exercise, *Notes to Myself,* are provided at the end of each unit. Students should be encouraged to share their journal entries with the class.

The material does not increase in difficulty as the book progresses, and no knowledge of previous lessons is required to complete later lessons. The lessons can be presented in any appropriate order taking into account the time constraints of the class and the needs and interests of the students.

In some exercises, more than one correct answer is possible. Answers will vary according to the students' experiences and level of English competency. Accept any correct response and encourage students to learn from the responses of others in the class.

If time allows, students may wish to create additional exercises patterned after those in this book. This procedure provides a useful learning experience both for those who create the material and those who utilize it as an added review.

1. BODY

Dictionary page 2

A. Look at the picture. Write *above*, *below*, or *between*.

1. The wrist is ___between___ the hand and the arm.

2. The leg is _____ the ankle.

3. The neck is _____ the head.

4. The waist is _____ the abdomen.

5. The shin is _____ the foot and the thigh.

6. The chest is _____ the stomach.

7. The shoulder is _____ the elbow.

8. The back is _____ the buttocks.

9. The knee is _____ the thigh and the shin.

10. The hip is _____ the stomach.

B. Write these words in alphabetical order.

elbow	1.	_ankle_
ankle	2.	_____
head	3.	_____
waist	4.	_____
buttocks	5.	_____
feet	6.	_____
shoulders	7.	_____
thigh	8.	_____
knee	9.	_____
neck	10.	_____

A. Cross out the word in each row that doesn't belong.

1.	throat	windpipe	esophagus	~~skin~~
2.	kneecap	shin	ribs	calf
3.	backbone	ribs	heart	breastbone
4.	brain	colon	small intestine	pancreas
5.	hand	forearm	anklebone	shoulder blade
6.	jaw	cheek	liver	skull
7.	blood	vein	artery	bones
8.	neck	stomach	spleen	liver

B. Write questions using words from the box. Begin each question with *What* or *Where*.

breastbone	stomach	esophagus	blood
windpipe	brain	veins	heart

1. <u>*What does your stomach do?*</u>

It digests your food.

2. _____?

It's in your veins and arteries.

3. _____?

It helps you think.

4. _____?

They carry blood to all parts of your body.

5. _____?

It's next to your lungs.

6. _____?

It carries air to your lungs.

7. _____?

It's over your heart.

8. _____?

It's in your throat.

A. Answer the questions using complete sentences.

1. Where do your tears come from?
   <u>My tears come from my eyes.</u>

2. Where are your teeth?
   _____

3. What do you wear on your finger?
   _____

4. What color are your eyes?
   _____

5. Where is your heel?
   _____

6. What part of your mouth helps you smile?
   _____

7. Where are your eyelashes?
   _____

8. What part of your face is most important to you? Why?
   _____

B. Complete the relationships using words from page 4 in the *Dictionary*.

1.	fingernail: finger	toenail: <u>toe</u>
2.	pupil: eye	teeth: _____
3.	ankle: foot	wrist: _____
4.	eyebrow: eye	moustache: _____
5.	thumb: hand	toe: _____
6.	ear: head	nose: _____
7.	sole: foot	palm: _____
8.	beard: chin	eyelashes: _____

A.   Look at the pictures and label the parts of the body. Then write the **verbs** that describe the actions in the pictures.

1. ___throw___   2. _____   3. _____

4. _____   5. _____   6. _____

7. _____   8. _____   9. _____

B.   Write the *-ing* form of the **verbs**.

I was just __thinking__ (think) about yesterday. While I was _____ (run) in
                1   2

the park and _____ (talk) to my friends, my sister was _____ (walk) around
             3   4

the garden. She was _____ (smell) the flowers and _____ (listen) to music
                    5   6

on her radio. When I returned home, she was _____ (stand) at
                                            7

the door. She was _____ (smile) and _____ (wave) to me.
                  8   9

C. Complete each sentence using a **verb** and a **noun**. Use each word once.

Verbs	Nouns
write	flower
listen	chair
walk	letter
~~drink~~	store
throw	mother
smell	~~milk~~
sit	ball
kiss	radio

1. _____ I drink a lot of milk _____ for breakfast.

2. Don't _____ in the park.

3. When I am alone, _____.

4. _____ in my yard.

5. _____ when I come home from school.

6. When I read, _____.

7. _____ to a friend.

8. When I need groceries, _____.

D. Complete the sentences using **verbs** from the box. Then write the new sentences.

write	think	kiss	bite	listen
talk	sit	taste	cry	throw

1. _____ the ball with your arm.   Throw the ball with your arm.

2. _____ the hot soup.   _____

3. _____ with your lips.   _____

4. _____ with your friends on the phone.   _____

5. _____ into the apple.   _____

6. _____ if it hurts.   _____

7. Always _____ before you speak.   _____

8. Don't _____ on a broken chair.   _____

9. _____ with your ears.   _____

10. _____ with the pencil on the paper.   _____

5

5. DESCRIBING PEOPLE: ADJECTIVES

A. Look at the pictures. Write the **adjectives** that are the *opposite* of the pictures. Use the words on page 6 of the **Dictionary**.

1. ____tall____
2. _____
3. _____
4. _____

5. _____
6. _____
7. _____
8. _____

B. Look at your classmates. Do a survey. Write a number in each box. Then complete the sentences below using *has* or *have*. (Change the first answer after you do your survey.)

	short hair	long hair
black	3	
blond		
white/gray		
brown		
red		
bald		

1. _Three people have_ short, black hair.
2. _____ long, black hair.
3. _____ short, blond hair.
4. _____ long, blond hair.
5. _____ short, white/gray hair.
6. _____ long, white/gray hair.
7. _____ short, brown hair.
8. _____ long, brown hair.
9. _____ short, red hair.
10. _____ long, red hair.
11. How many people are bald?_____

_____ no hair.

6

A. Complete the family tree. Fill in the names of your relatives. Tell a partner about your family.

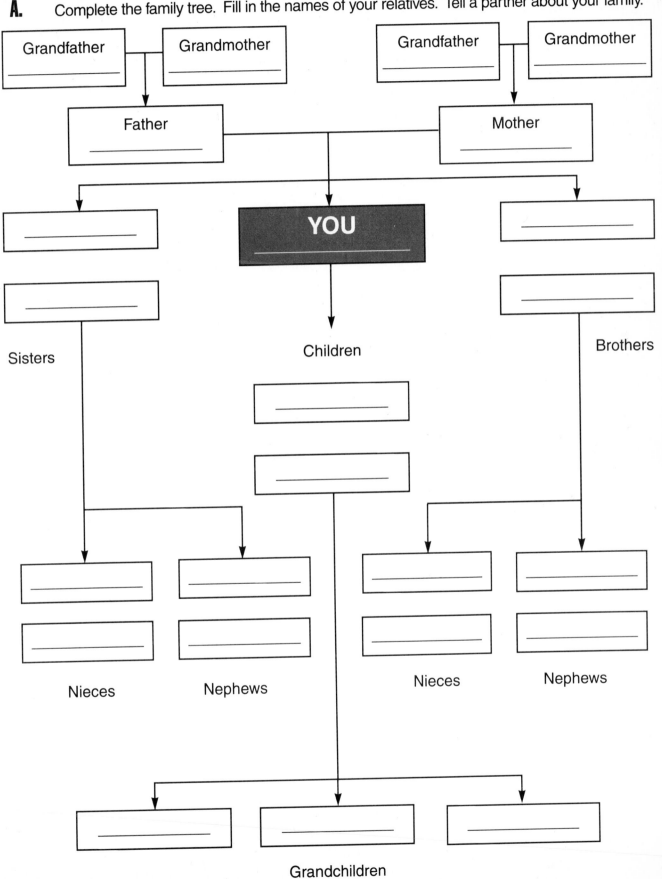

A. Complete the crossword puzzle using words from page 8 in the **Dictionary**.

Across

1. Your cat is lost.
3. You wish you had your friend's new bike.
5. Your wallet is stolen.
7. You're planning a wedding.
9. You receive an unexpected bouquet of flowers.
10. Someone hit your car.

Down

2. Someone is following you.
4. You see a man sleeping in the street.
6. No one remembers your birthday.
8. Your child is graduating from high school.

A.

Vocabulary Practice

How many words do you remember from this unit? Answer the questions using as many vocabulary words as you can without looking in the *Dictionary*. Then compare your list with another student's.

Who are they?

father

What are they doing?

walking

What are you doing?

B.   **Notes to Myself**

NoTes

Topic: *My Family*

Date: _____

What do you look like? Do you have any sisters or brothers? Describe yourself and your family using adjectives from page 6 of the *Dictionary*.

_____

_____

_____

_____

_____

_____

_____

Write about a recent sad or happy event in your life. Include some of the words from page 8 of the *Dictionary*.

_____

_____

_____

_____

_____

_____

9. OUTER CLOTHING

Dictionary page 9

A. Study the picture on page 9 in the ***Dictionary***. Then answer these questions.

1. You're going to Alaska, where it's very cold and snowy. What will you wear?

   _____hat_____   _____   _____

2. You're going hiking in the mountains. What will you wear?

   _____   _____   _____

3. You're going to Seattle, where it's cool and very rainy. What will you wear?

   _____   _____   _____

4. You're a police officer, and you work outside most of the time. What do you wear?

   _____   _____   _____

B. Answer these questions using complete sentences.

What is the difference between:

1. a coat and a jacket?
   A coat is longer than a jacket. _____

2. a hat and ear muffs?

   _____

3. shoes and boots?

   _____

4. a turtleneck and a V-neck?

   _____

5. a down vest and a sweater?

   _____

A. Match each item with a part of the body.

<u> 2 </u> pants   **1.** face

_____ glasses   **2.** legs

_____ loafer   **3.** chest

_____ belt   **4.** foot

_____ collar   **5.** neck

_____ vest   **6.** waist

B. Match each item in Column A with an item in Column B.

A		**B**
<u> 5 </u> belt		**1.** suit jacket
_____ handkerchief		**2.** wallet
_____ tie		**3.** shirt
_____ undershirt		**4.** briefs
_____ money		**5.** slacks

C. Read the paragraphs. Then circle the letters of the correct answers.

1. Kenji is wearing a dark suit, a white shirt, a new tie, and his new shoes. He has just looked at his watch. He doesn't want to be late. He puts on his overcoat. He is probably going to

    a. play tennis.
    b. attend a wedding.
    c. cook dinner.

2. Robert is wearing a bathrobe and slippers. He has just put his suit and shoes in the closet. He has a lot of reading to do for his meeting in the morning. He is probably going to

    a. play soccer.
    b. go to a party.
    c. stay home.

3. Pedro is wearing long johns, heavy pants, and a long-sleeved shirt. He has just bought warm socks, a down vest, earmuffs, and mittens. He is probably going to

    a. go skiing.
    b. play cards.
    c. go to bed.

4. Bill is wearing a shirt, a tie, slacks, and a sport coat. His wallet is in his pocket and his briefcase is in his hand. He is probably going to

    a. visit a museum.
    b. watch a baseball game.
    c. go to work.

D. Word Search: Find twelve items of men's clothing from page 10 in the **Dictionary**. Circle them. Then answer the questions using the circled words.

S	V	E	S	T	D	F	L	J	T
N	K	P	U	G	I	Q	O	N	I
E	B	R	I	E	F	C	A	S	E
A	L	O	T	H	C	O	F	P	S
K	E	M	H	E	E	L	E	A	H
E	B	B	E	L	T	L	R	N	I
R	P	A	J	A	M	A	S	T	R
S	L	I	P	P	E	R	A	S	T

1. What do you need to hold up your pants? _a_
2. What goes under your collar? _a_
3. What holds important papers? _a_
4. What kind of shoes do you wear to go jogging? _____
5. What do you wear to sleep? _____

E. Circle the word in each row that doesn't belong. Then give a reason.

1. sneaker   shirt   (wallet)   slacks
   You can't wear a wallet. _____

2. briefs   tie   boxer shorts   long johns
   _____

3. money   handkerchief   briefcase   wallet
   _____

4. slippers   pants   loafers   sneakers
   _____

5. suit jacket   bathrobe   tie   shirt
   _____

6. pajamas   bathrobe   suit jacket   slippers
   _____

A.   Look at the picture. Complete the conversation using words from page 11 in the *Dictionary*.

Mother: I'm going shopping. Do you want to go to the _____clothing_____ store with me?
                                                                    1

little girl: Yes, Mommy. I want to go shopping with you. Please help me take off my

                  _____ .
                         2

Mother: O.K. I'll help you. You can go with me if you get dressed.

little girl: I'll wear my _____ under my dress and I will take my cardigan
                                        3

                  _____ . I don't want to get cold.
                         4

big sister: I want to go, too. If I wear my _____ and my _____ ,
                                                          5   **6**

              will I be warm enough?

Mother: Yes. You can go if you help your sister get dressed.

big sister: Great! Mommy, don't forget to put money in your _____ .
                                                                          7

B.   Work with a partner. Look at the picture above and create your own conversation.

C. Create advertisements. Write a few words in each box to describe the item of clothing.

Carry Your Money in Style Buy a new *purse*.	--------------- --------------- Buy new *tights*.	--------------- --------------- Buy a new *barrette*.
--------------- --------------- Buy new *underwear*.	--------------- --------------- Buy a new pair of *high heels*.	--------------- --------------- Buy a new *nightgown*.

D. Look at page 11 in the **Dictionary**. Write *is, are, isn't,* or *aren't*.

1. There __aren't__ any socks on the bed.

2. There _____ clothes in the closet.

3. The little girl _____ wearing a skirt.

4. No one _____ looking in the mirror.

5. The mother _____ wearing a suit.

6. The ankle socks _____ very big.

7. Three people _____ in the room.

8. There _____ a purse on the floor.

E. Circle *before* or *after*. Then complete the sentence.

1. You should put on a skirt (before, (after)) ___you put on your___ slip.

2. You have to take off your nightgown (before, after) _____ school.

3. You usually put money in your purse (before, after) _____ shopping.

4. You can button a blouse (before, after) _____ camisole.

5. Wash your dirty clothes (before, after) _____ in your closet.

6. You always put on your underwear (before, after) _____ clothes.

15

12. COLORS AND PATTERNS

A. What is your favorite color? Fill in the chart. Tell a partner about your choice. Change the first answer.

My favorite color for …

1. my bedroom walls	blue
2. a shirt or blouse	
3. a car	
4. underwear	
5. frames for my eyeglasses	
6. a bathing suit	
7. an overcoat	
8. balloon	
9. roses	
10. shoes	

B. Look at page 12 in the ***Dictionary***. Fill in the missing colors in the following descriptions.

1. Number 17 is solid __yellow__ .

2. Number 18 has _____ and _____ stripes.

3. Number 19 is _____ and _____ checked.

4. Number 20 is a _____, _____, _____, and _____ plaid.

5. Number 21 is a _____ and _____ paisley print.

6. Number 22 has _____ polka dots on a _____ background.

7. Number 23 has _____ flowers on a _____ background.

C. Describe the clothes five classmates are wearing.

1. Thanos is wearing a red and black paisley tie.

2. _____

3. _____

4. _____

5. _____

6. _____

A. These items are for sale in a department store. Answer the questions using the information below.

Jewelry	
Wedding ring	$480
Watch	$250
Pearls	$180
Bracelet	$ 90
Tie clip	$ 75

Cosmetics	
Lipstick	$ 15
Mascara	$ 12
Powder	$ 10
Rouge	$ 8
Eyeliner	$ 6

Toiletries	
Perfume	$ 48
After-shave lotion	$ 25
Shampoo	$ 12
Razor	$ 10
Razor blades	$ 6

1. Pablo wants to get a gift for his girlfriend. He only has $50. What can he buy?
   Perfume or _____

2. Sonja always complains that her lips are dry. What should she put on them?
   _____ She has $20 in her wallet. Can she buy this item?
   _____

3. Robert is going camping. He doesn't want to grow a beard. What toiletries will he
   need to buy? _____ and _____ How much will these
   items cost? $_____

4. Susan and Billy are going shopping together. They both want to buy something
   that makes them smell good. What can Susan buy? _____
   What can Billy buy? _____ Can they buy these items if
   they each have $50? _____

5. Tom has no money. He is going to borrow $200 from his mother. Then he is going
   to meet his brother at the department store. Tom knows his mother's watch is
   broken and he wants to buy her another one. Should Tom buy her a watch?
   _____ Why or why not? _____
   _____

6. Mrs. Jones has two daughters. One daughter asked for a piece of jewelry to wear
   around her neck. The other daughter asked for a piece of jewelry to wear around
   her wrist. Mrs. Jones has $300 dollars in her purse. What items can she buy at
   the department store? _____

7. **You have just won $500!** You can now buy what you need or what you have
   been wishing for. Write a few sentences telling how you will spend your money.

   _____
   _____

B. Circle the letters of the words that complete the relationships.

1. face: soap   hair:
   - **a.** shampoo *(circled)*
   - **b.** razor
   - **c.** cotton balls
   - **d.** comb

2. lips: lipstick   eyelashes:
   - **a.** bobby pins
   - **b.** powder
   - **c.** mascara
   - **d.** soap

3. woman: perfume   man:
   - **a.** shampoo
   - **b.** shaving cream
   - **c.** after-shave
   - **d.** soap

4. neck: necklace   wrist:
   - **a.** clasp
   - **b.** bracelet
   - **c.** ring
   - **d.** pin

5. cheek: rouge   fingernail:
   - **a.** shampoo
   - **b.** curlers
   - **c.** tweezers
   - **d.** nail polish

6. nails: emery board   face:
   - **a.** tweezers
   - **b.** razor
   - **c.** nail clipper
   - **d.** comb

C. **Emergency!** You are far away from home. The airline has lost your suitcase. Make a list of five toiletries you must buy immediately.

_____   _____

_____   _____

_____

A.   Vocabulary Practice

How many words do you remember from this unit? Answer the questions using as many vocabulary words as you can without looking in the *Dictionary*. Then compare your list with another student's.

What are they wearing? Describe their clothes. What are you wearing? Add the items to your list below.

striped pants

What toiletries and cosmetics did you use this morning?

B. Notes to Myself

Topic: *How I Look*

Date: _____

What are you wearing today? Use the color and pattern vocabulary words to describe your clothing.

_____

_____

_____

_____

_____

_____

You have been invited to go see a football game in Chicago this winter. Describe how you will need to dress to keep warm. Use vocabulary words from page 9 in the *Dictionary*.

_____

_____

_____

_____

_____

_____

15. HOUSING

Dictionary pages 14—16

A. Look at the ads. Put a check (✔) in the appropriate column.

> **SOLIDLY CONSTRUCTED** Ranch on beautiful corner property, walk to elem. school, 3 bdrms, 2 bths, modern eat-in-kit + large fam rm.

> **PRIVATE ESTATE COMPOUND.** Long drive to dramatic setting. Over 7 acres in top estate area. Beautifully built to take advantage of distant views. Two guest houses. Stable. Pond. Landscaping. Magnificent!

Which house would you think of buying if . . .	Ranch	Estate
1. you owned horses.		
2. you had young, school-age children.		
3. you wanted the rooms on one floor.		
4. your family and friends visit on the weekends.		
5. you might consider building a swimming pool.		
6. you didn't want to live near city noise and traffic.		

B. Study the two pictures. Write four more sentences telling how the houses are different.

A

B

1. _____ House A has a lamp post but house B doesn't. _____

2. _____

3. _____

4. _____

5. _____

C. Read the following conversations. Then tell where Mr. and Mrs. Rivera are.

		The Rivera's are . . .
1.	**Mr. Rivera:** Maybe they aren't home right now. **Mrs. Rivera:** Ring the doorbell again.	on _the porch_ .
2.	**Mr. Rivera:** These clothes have been washed. **Mrs. Rivera:** O.K. I'll put them in the dryer.	in _____ .
3.	**Mr. Rivera:** Have you finished your bath? **Mrs. Rivera:** No. I'll be out in a minute.	in _____ .
4.	**Mr. Rivera:** The baby is still crying. **Mrs. Rivera:** Let's take her out of the crib.	in _____ .
5.	**Mr. Rivera:** It sure is hot up here! **Mrs. Rivera:** Let's finish with this antenna and go back inside.	on _____ .
6.	**Mr. Rivera:** There are too many things in here. **Mrs. Rivera:** I know. There isn't room for the car.	in _____ .
7.	**Mr. Rivera:** Where's the milk? **Mrs. Rivera:** It's right there in the refrigerator.	in _____ .
8.	**Mr. Rivera:** Please turn the light off. **Mrs. Rivera:** O.K. I'm ready to go to sleep, too.	in _____ .

D. Answer these questions about your home.

1. How many rooms are there in your home? _____
2. Do you have a hall or foyer? _____
3. How many bedrooms are there? _____
4. How many bathrooms? _____
5. Does your home have a porch or a balcony? _____
6. What room do you eat your meals in? _____
7. What room do you do your homework in? _____
8. Do you have a television? _____
9. Where is it? _____
10. Do you have an antenna on the roof? _____

E. Circle the word in each row that doesn't belong. Give a reason for your choice.

1. roof   chimney   attic   (floor)

   The floor isn't at the top of the house.

2. street   family room   sidewalk   driveway

   _____

3. door   doorbell   garage   steps

   _____

4. closet   antenna   shutters   doorbell

   _____

5. fence   gate   tool room   yard

   _____

6. kitchen   nursery   den   doorbell

   _____

F. Complete the chart using words from page 16 in the *Dictionary.*

House Rules	
Do	**Don't**
1. Shut the _door_ and lock it when you leave the house.	1. Keep the television on in the _____.
2. Turn off the water in the _____ after you brush your teeth.	2. Play on the _____ of the house.
3. Park your car in the _____.	3. Run up and down the _____ inside the house.
4. Wash your clothes in the _____ _____.	4. Leave your clothes all over the _____ floor.
5. Put the baby to sleep in the _____.	5. Play in the _____ when it's dark.

A.   The woman in the picture on page 17 in the *Dictionary* is having problems with some
things in her living room. She wants someone to repair them. Read her notes and tell
what she wants each person to repair.

> ●   1. It doesn't tell the correct time anymore.
>
>   2. It doesn't sound right when I play it.
>
>   3. It lets smoke come into the room.
>
>   4. The glass is broken and rain comes in.
>
>   5. It falls over when I put my feet on it.
> ●
>   6. It doesn't ring loud enough. I can't hear it.

1. _____clock_____   4. _____

2. _____   5. _____

3. _____   6. _____

B.   Look at page 17 in the *Dictionary*. Complete the sentences using **prepositions** from
the box.

in	under	above	next to	behind	in front of

1. The wooden logs are ___in___
   the fireplace.

2. The cat is resting _____
   the hearth.

3. The window is _____
   the blinds.

4. The plant is _____ the staircase.

5. The painting is hanging _____
   the clock.

6. The telephone directory is _____
   the telephone.

7. The end table is _____
   the sofa.

8. The woman is sitting _____
   the armchair.

A. Look at page 18 in the ***Dictionary***. Cross out the word that doesn't belong in each sentence. Then rewrite the sentence using the correct word.

1. The man is putting the ice tray into the ~~dishwasher.~~

   The man is putting the ice tray into the freezer.

2. The stove is under the sink.

   _____

3. The dishes and silverware are drying in the broiler.

   _____

4. The woman is using a blender to make cookies.

   _____

5. The sauce pan is on the cutting board.

   _____

6. The dog is watching the steaks on the counter.

   _____

B. What items in the kitchen do you need to do these jobs? Choose the words from page 18 in the ***Dictionary*** to show which things you could use.

To . . .	use a . . .		
1. make bacon and eggs,	*frying pan*	and a	.
2. clean the pots and pans,		and a	.
3. make a cherry pie,		and a	.
4. make ice,		and an	.
5. mix flour and milk,		and a	.
6. cook vegetables,		and a	.

C. Look at page 18 in the *Dictionary*. Write a letter in front of each number to show where you can find the item.

a. near the sink

b. far away from the refrigerator

c. in a cabinet

d. on a counter

_a_ **1.** microwave oven

____ **2.** electric mixer

____ **3.** stool

____ **4.** faucet

____ **5.** can opener

____ **6.** dish drainer

____ **7.** wastebasket

____ **8.** dish towel

____ **9.** dishcloth

____ **10.** rolling pin

____ **11.** cups and saucers

____ **12.** dog

D. Complete this survey by checking the correct column.

	already have	plan to buy	will never buy
dishwasher			
electric mixer			
garbage disposal			
dish drainer			
blender			
whisk			
microwave oven			
colander			
electric can opener			

A. Complete the story and crossword puzzle using the words on page 19 of the *Dictionary*.

Setting the Table

No matter how many people come to dinner it is important to set the

___table___ properly. Place a tablecloth over the table and put a chair where
5A

each person sits. In the center of the table place two candlesticks with tall

_____. Put a _____ on the table in front of each chair. On the
7A 10A

left side of the plate put a _____. You can put a napkin under the
12A

fork or you can place a napkin in a _____ ring above the plate. Put a
9D

_____ on the right side of the plate and a _____
6D 8D

next to the knife. Place a glass near the spoon and knife. Then place salt and

_____ shakers and a _____ of water or soda anywhere
11A 2D

on the table. Put cups and _____, and a _____
4D 1A

and creamer on the table after the main course. When coffee and tea are ready,

bring out the _____ _____, the _____, and dessert.
3D 13A

A. Use words from page 20 in the **Dictionary** to help Roberto read the note from his mother.

Dear Roberto,

Before you leave, please turn off the ___air___ ___conditioner___
1
and open the _____ . Please put your _____ and _____ in the
2   3   4
bathroom, and your socks in the _____ drawer. Put the book
5
back on the _____ . Hang your pajamas in the _____ and
6   7
close the door. The weather is warm so you can take your _____
8
off the bed. Put it in the _____ . Have a nice day.
9
Love,

Mom

B. Look at the picture in Exercise A. Circle *is* or *are*. Then write the correct forms of the **verbs** to complete the sentences.

1. Someone ((is), are) ___knocking___ at the door. (knock)

2. The sock (is, are) _____ on the floor. (fall)

3. The boy (is, are) _____ . (smile)

4. The boy's shirt (is, are) _____ in the closet. (hang)

5. The boy (is, are) _____ about his chores. (think)

6. The doorbell (is, are) _____ . (ring)

C. Complete each sentence.

_C_ **1.** An alarm clock
    2. An air conditioner
    3. A frame
    4. A carpet
    5. A fitted sheet
    6. A comforter

a. goes with a picture.
b. covers the mattress.
c. makes a loud noise.
d. is for cold weather.
e. keeps you cool.
f. covers the floor.

D. Finish the comparisons. Circle the letter of the correct answer.

1.	pillow: pillowcase	mattress:	a. floor **(b.)** fitted sheet c. bed d. comb
2.	alarm clock: night stand	book:	a. closet b. pillow c. shelf d. lamp
3.	dresser: mirror	bed:	a. headboard b. bureau c. lamp shade d. door
4.	curtains: window	lamp shade:	a. lamp b. closet c. shelf d. rug
5.	carpet: floor	bedspread:	a. hairbrush b. drawer c. bed d. light switch
6.	clothes: closet	socks:	a. wall b. shelf c. ceiling d. drawer

A. Look at the nursery on page 21 in the **Dictionary**. Compare the items and people using the words in the box. Use each word only once.

higher	faster	noisier	wider
busier	bigger	taller	smaller

1. The baby is _____bigger_____ than the doll.

2. The crib is _____ than the changing table.

3. The mother is _____ than the boy.

4. The swing is _____ than the toy chest.

5. The stuffed animal is _____ than the baby.

6. The stroller can move _____ than the walker.

7. The baby is _____ than his brother.

8. The mother is _____ than her children.

B. You are going to take the baby to the park for three hours. What six items from the nursery would you choose to take?

_____   _____   _____

_____   _____   _____

C. Look at the baby's toys in the nursery on page 21 in the **Dictionary**. Then answer the questions using complete sentences.

What is the difference between:

1. a crib and a playpen?

   A crib is for sleeping and a playpen is for playing.

2. a stroller and a high chair?

   _____

3. a swing and a walker?

   _____

4. a pacifier and a nipple?

   _____

A. What should each person do? Read each of the sentences below. Then write a short sentence telling the person what to do.

1. I finished my bath. I don't want to get the floor wet.

   Use the bath mat.

2. The water doesn't stay in the tub.

   _____

3. I don't like to sit in the bathtub.

   _____

4. My face is wet.

   _____

5. These clothes are dirty. They need to be washed.

   _____

B. Name each item pictured below. Then tell where you find it in the bathroom.

1.  _a faucet_   _on sinks, bathtubs, showers_

2. _____   _____

3. 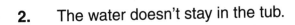 _____   _____

4.  _____   _____

A. Make sentences using words from Column A, Column B, and Column C.

Column A (Nouns)	Column B (Verbs)	Column C (Nouns)
~~washing machine~~	holds	floor
dryer	~~cleans~~	~~clothes~~
furnace	carries	water
clothesline	heats	electricity
bucket	dries	house
vacuum cleaner		
extension cord		
dust mop		

1. The washing machine cleans clothes.

2. _____

3. _____

4. _____

5. _____

6. _____

7. _____

8. _____

B. Read the following conversations. Then tell what Mr. and Mrs. Lopez are doing.

1. **Mr. Lopez:** Did you put the bleach in yet?
   Mrs. Lopez: Yes, I did. Give me the fabric softener, please.
   They're washing clothes.

2. **Mr. Lopez:** This room looks terrible.
   Mrs. Lopez: I know. Here's the paint can and roller.

   _____

3. **Mr. Lopez:** Does the cord on the iron reach the outlet?
   Mrs. Lopez: No, it doesn't. Can you find an extension cord?

   _____

4. **Mr. Lopez:** Do you want to use the broom and dustpan?
   Mrs. Lopez: No. I think I'll use the vacuum cleaner.

   _____

C. Number the following items from 1 to 7 to show the order in which you do laundry.

_____ Put the clothes in the dryer.   _____ Put the clean clothes in the laundry basket.

Start the washer.   _____ Take the clothes out of the washer.

_____ Take the clothes out of the dryer.   _____ Start the dryer.

_____ Put the clothes in the washer.   _____ Add the laundry detergent.

D. There is a problem in each picture. What items from page 23 in the **Dictionary** could you use to solve each problem?

1. _____ bleach _____
_____ laundry detergent _____
_____ washing machine _____
_____

2. _____
_____
_____

3. _____
_____
_____
_____

4. _____
_____
_____

5. _____
_____
_____
_____

6. _____
_____
_____

A. Complete the story using words from page 24 in the *Dictionary*.

Friday Afternoon

It's Friday afternoon. Mrs. Carter is standing on her _____*deck*_____ cooking

<u>1</u>

fish on the _____. She is starting the fire with _____ and

<u>2</u> <u>3</u>

_____. Billy is mowing the lawn and Sally is using the _____

<u>4</u> <u>5</u>

to spray water on the cat. Alex is jumping off the _____ into the

<u>6</u>

_____ to stay cool.

<u>7</u>

Soon Mr. Carter will be home. First he'll do some work in the vegetable garden

using the _____ and the _____. Then he'll pick some flowers

<u>8</u> <u>9</u>

from the _____ and give them to Mrs. Carter. After that, he'll lie down on

<u>10</u>

a _____ and watch the children play. The family will have dinner on the

<u>11</u>

_____.

<u>12</u>

B. Rewrite the sentences below using the **conjunctions** from the box. Use each word only once.

because	and	or	but	yet

1. The sun is shining. The air is warm.
   <u>The sun is shining **and** the air is warm.</u>

2. My mother is cooking fish. I'm not hungry now.

   _____

3. My father is mowing the grass. It's too long.

   _____

4. Drink the iced tea. Eat the fruit.

   _____

5. The garden needs weeding. The pool needs cleaning.

   _____

6. It might rain soon. Everyone seems happy.

   _____

C. You need to be careful in the yard. Here are some warnings. Tell what each warning is talking about.

1. Don't put your hand there. It's hot!

   the barbecue

2. Watch the baby. He might fall in.

   _____

3. Don't walk in there. You'll kill the flowers.

   _____

4. Keep it away from the barbecue. It might start a fire.

   _____

5. That little boy shouldn't use it. He's not strong enough.

   _____

6. Stop doing that! The cat doesn't like it.

   _____

D. Work with a partner. Read each of these suggestions and check *Like* or *Dislike*. Does your partner like to do the same things you do?

	Like	Dislike
Swim in a swimming pool		
Dive from a diving board		
Cook on a barbecue		
Eat barbecued food		
Eat vegetables		
Plant a flower garden		
Sit in the hot sun		
Climb a tree		
Mow a lawn		
Play with children		

A. Study the **verbs** on page 25 of the *Dictionary*. Then write short sentences using these **verbs**.

1. ___Knock on the door.___

2. _____

3. _____

4. _____

5. _____

B. Answer the questions using complete sentences.

1. What does Lee do when the windows are dirty?

   ___He cleans the windows._____

2. What does Carlos do before he leaves the house?

   _____

3. What do you do when the doorbell rings?

   _____

4. What does Stella do when the carpet is dirty?

   _____

5. What do you do when the grass is too long?

   _____

C. Complete the crossword puzzle using words from page 25 in the **Dictionary**.

		1				2 P	A	I	N	3 T	
		4									
5				6							
		7					8		9		
					10						
11											

Across

2. Do you use a roller or a brush when you _paint_?

4. We must _____ this chair before we paint it.

5. Don't forget to _____ when you leave the house.
   (three words)

7. The best way to clean a carpet is to _____ it.

10. When the floor gets dirty, _____ it with a broom.

11. Before you go in the house, please _____ the bell.

Down

1. It's dark in here. Please _____ the lights.
   (two words)

3. I'm going to bed. Will you _____ the lights?
   (two words)

6. Did someone _____ on the door?

7. I'm going to _____ my sister at her house.

8. The grass is too long. I need to_____ it today.

9. This place is a mess! Will you help me _____ it?

A.   **Vocabulary Practice**

How many words do you remember from this unit? Answer the questions using as many vocabulary words as you can without looking in the **Dictionary**. Then compare your list with another student's.

What rooms and items inside the house do you recognize? What do you see outside the house? What are the children doing?

outside
roof

inside
nursery

activities
painting

Write the names of parts of your house or home that are not shown in the picture above.

B.

Notes to Myself

NoTes

Topic: *Where I Live*

Date: _____

Where do you live? How many rooms are in your home or apartment? Do you have a place to study? Watch television? Do laundry? Eat? Relax? What are your jobs or responsibilities around the house? Use the words in this unit to help describe your style of living.

_____

_____

_____

_____

_____

_____

_____

What is your *favorite* room or part of your house or apartment? Why? Use the words in this unit to help explain why this area of your house is so special.

_____

_____

_____

_____

_____

_____

26. **FRUIT**

Dictionary pages 26–27

Complete the sentences using the information in the picture.

A. Write *more* or *less*.

1. You can buy ___more___ pears than apples for 89¢.

2. Watermelon is _____ expensive than honeydew melon.

3. There are _____ than six kinds of fruit in the fruit stand.

4. Sam says he needs _____ grapes for the fruit stand.

5. Cantaloupe is _____ per pound than honeydew.

6. The bananas could be _____ ripe.

7. Grapes cost _____ per pound than any melon.

8. Six bananas cost _____ than $1.00.

B. Write the **plural** form for these fruits.

1. apple ___apples___   5. raisin _____

2. strawberry_____   6. cherry _____

3. lemon _____   7. pear _____

4. peach _____   8. banana _____

C. Read the following conversations. Then tell what fruit Nora and David are talking about.

1. **Nora:** Ask them to put a hole in one side.
    David: Good idea. Then we can drink the milk.

    It's a coconut.

2. **Nora:** I love this red melon!
    David: I do, too. But don't eat the pits!

    _____

3. **Nora:** Oh! This tastes sour!
    David: Don't drink it. Put some of the juice in your tea.

    _____

4. **Nora:** What is that red stuff in the jar?
    David: It's my favorite kind of jam.

    _____

5. **Nora:** These little fruits make a great snack.
    David: Have you ever put them in your cereal?

    _____

D. Read the recipe below for fruit salad. Rewrite the instructions in the correct order.

Marshmallow Fruit Salad

1/2 cup strawberries, quartered
8 large marshmallows
2 bananas, mashed
1/2 cup crushed pineapple

1/2 cup whipping cream
1/4 cup mayonnaise
1/2 cup cubed peaches

To serve, cut into quarters. Allow the marshmallows to cool. Stir mayonnaise and whipping cream into the fruit. Add strawberries, mashed bananas, pineapple, and peaches. Melt the marshmallows. Defrost. Pour into a freezing tray and freeze. Top each piece with marshmallows.

Melt the marshmallows. _____

_____

_____

_____

_____

A. Look at the pictures of food. List some vegetables you can use to make each one.

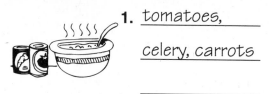

1. *tomatoes,*
   celery, carrots

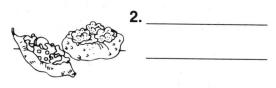

2. _____
   _____
   _____

3. _____
   _____
   _____

4. _____
   _____
   _____

B. Complete the crossword puzzle using the names of vegetables on pages 28 and 29 in the **Dictionary.**

		1								
2					3					
								4		
V	E	G	E	T	A	B	L	E	S	
	5				6					
		7								

Across

1. A bowl of mixed vegetables is a _____.

2. Cut _____ into long or short orange "sticks."

5. _____ beans are small, red beans.

7. A hard, juicy, white vegetable with green skin is a _____.

Down

1. Green beans are also called _____ beans.

3. Red, round, juicy _____ can be home-grown.

4. Green and leafy describes _____

6. A sweet, orange potato is a _____.

C. Complete the lists.

Vegetables that go in salad	Vegetables you must cook before eating.
1. _lettuce_	1. _potatoes_
2. _____	2. _____
3. _____	3. _____
4. _____	4. _____
5. _____	5. _____

Vegetables you don't like
1. _____
2. _____
3. _____
4. _____
5. _____

D. Check the vegetables that are grown in your native country. Then check the vegetables you have eaten in the past month.

	Native country	I have eaten it this month
avocado		
eggplant		
chili peppers		
soy beans		
yams		
broccoli		
okra		
celery		
corn		
artichokes		
spinach		
squash		
radish		

A. Complete the conversation using **question words** from the box.

who	who's	what	what's	where	where's
	how		when		why

Dining Out

Mother: ___Who's___ hungry?
1

Girl: I am.

Boy: _____ on the menu?
2

Mother: Meat, fish, and chicken.

Girl: _____ the cheapest?
3

Boy: _____ cares?
4

Waiter: _____ ready to order?
5

Girl: _____ can you make fast?
6

Waiter: The fish takes the least amount of time. _____ wants to
7
order now?

Mother: I'll have lamb chops.

Waiter: _____ do you want them
8
cooked?

Mother: Medium rare. _____
9
long will it take?

Waiter: It will take about . . .

Girl: _____ the bathroom?
10

Waiter: In the back of the restaurant.

Girl: _____ wants to go with me?
11

Mother: You're old enough to go by yourself.

Boy: _____ will our food be
12
ready?

Waiter: _____ is everybody in such
13
a hurry?

Mother: We're just very tired. It's been a long day.

Waiter: The food will be out in fifteen minutes.

Girl: _____ my food?
14

Mother: Sit down. It will be out soon.

Boy: _____ are you always so
15
cranky?

Girl: I'm only seven years old.

Mother: And we're ALL very tired.

Waiter: Here's your dinner.
_____ ready to eat?
16

Boy/Girl: I am.

Mother: Me too!!

B. Work with a partner. Pretend you're in a restaurant. Create your own conversation.

44

Study the **bar graph**. Explain the eating habits of Paul's family during the past two years.

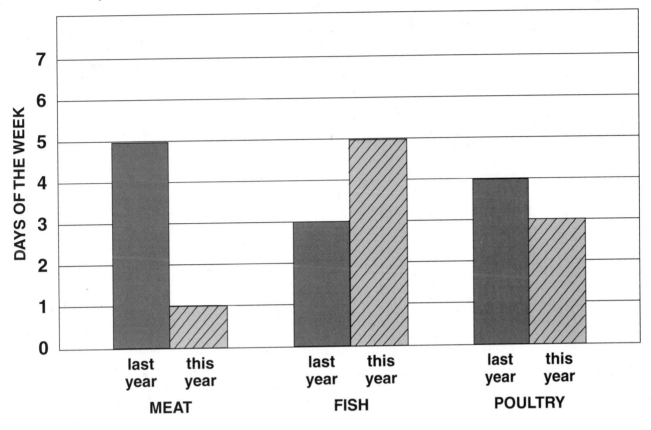

C. Answer the questions using the words *meat, fish,* or *poultry.*

1. What did Paul's family eat least last year? _____fish_____

2. What did Paul's family eat most last year? _____

3. What food do they eat five times a week this year? _____

4. What food has Paul's family almost stopped eating this year? _____

5. What food is eaten the most this year? _____

6. What food did Paul's family stop eating the least amount over the two years? _____

D. Write **T** for True or **F** for False.

___F___ 1. Paul's family ate meat seven times a week last year.

_____ 2. Paul's family is eating as much poultry this year as fish last year.

_____ 3. Paul's family is eating much less fish this year than last year.

_____ 4. Paul's family seems to enjoy fish.

_____ 5. Steaks, lamb chops, and bacon are popular foods in Paul's house this year.

_____ 6. Paul's family now cooks fish five times a week.

A. Cross out the word that doesn't belong in each sentence. Then rewrite the sentence using the correct word.

1. My favorite part of the ~~oyster~~ is the drumstick.

   <u>My favorite part of the chicken is the drumstick.</u>

2. Amos loves crab steak.

   _____

3. I love clams and scallops served in a shell.

   _____

4. When I'm on a diet, I enjoy a can of perch for lunch.

   _____

5. I'd like a fillet of lobster, please.

   _____

B. Complete the poems using the words on page 31 in the **Dictionary**.

Take some **time**.
Find a word to **rhyme**.

1. A little bird is called a *wren*.
   A female chicken is a ___hen___ .

2. In the water you may have to *search*
   To find a fish called a _____ .

3. For dessert you eat delicious *cake*.
   For the main course you cook a
   halibut _____ .

4. The chicken has a bony *chest*.
   It's the white meat and it's called
   the _____ .

5. This fish has legs to crawl and *grab*.
   It's known to some as a
   soft-shelled _____ .

6. Uncooked these tails feel a little *limp*.
   Cooked just right, they are tasty
   pink _____ .

C. Answer the following questions using complete sentences.

1. What is your favorite part of the chicken? Why?

   _____

2. What kind of fish do you like best? Why?

   _____

A. Read **Dave's Specials**. Write the foods that are being described. Then complete the menu by writing two more descriptions of items on pages 32 and 33 in the **Dictionary**.

DAVE'S SPECIALS

1. Great with butter and jelly!
2. Scrambled or fried.
3. Fresh from the ocean.
4. A sandwich big enough for two.
5. Mashed or baked. Your choice!
6. Crispy fried—white meat only!
7.
8.

1. _____toast_____   5. _____

2. _____   6. _____

3. _____   7. _____

4. _____   8. _____

B. How do you like to eat each of these foods? Write the words *hot, room temperature,* or *cold*.

1. toast _____hot_____   7. mashed potatoes _____

2. cereal _____   8. bagels _____

3. meat loaf _____   9. salad _____

4. pretzels _____   10. fried chicken _____

5. burritos _____   11. fruit salad _____

6. peanuts _____   12. pizza _____

C. The items below are "toppings" for common foods. Find the foods on pages 32 and 33 in the **Dictionary**. Write the words below.

1. ketchup _____french fries, hamburger_____

2. mayonnaise _____

3. mustard _____

4. butter _____

5. gravy _____

6. jelly _____

7. relish _____

D. Some "American" foods came from other countries. Which country do you think invented each food?

Mexico		Italy		China		England
	the U.S.A.		Germany		France	

1. pizza _____Italy_____   8. fried chicken _____

2. egg rolls _____   9. pretzels _____

3. french fries _____   10. burritos _____

4. pancakes _____   11. spaghetti _____

5. noodles _____   12. muffins _____

6. tacos _____   13. rice _____

7. soup _____   14. waffles _____

E. Finish the conversation with a friend.

You: It's almost noon. Are you hungry?

Your friend: Starving! I had a very early breakfast.

You: What do you feel like eating for lunch?

Your friend: I'd love _____

_____

A. Look at page 34 in the **Dictionary**. Then answer the questions using the names of desserts.

1. Carol can't eat chocolate. What desserts can she eat?

pie, sherbet, strawberry shortcake

2. Paul can't have any milk. What desserts can he eat?

3. Which desserts are made with ice cream?

4. Which desserts have the most chocolate in them?

5. Which desserts are "finger foods"?

6. Which desserts must be kept cold?

7. Which desserts are good when they're served warm?

B. Complete the statements using the dessert menu.

DESSERT MENU

$1.25

$ .65 each

$1.45

$ .85

.95

1. I'm on a low-fat diet. I can order _____ or _____ .

2. I want a "little something sweet" with my coffee. I think I'll have a _____ .

3. I'd love some fruit, but I have a craving for whipped cream. I'll try the _____ .

4. I only have $1.30 in my pocket. If I want cake, I guess I'll have to order the _____ .

5. These prices are quite reasonable. The cheapest dessert on the menu is _____ . The most expensive is _____ .

6. My aunt would love these desserts. She'd definitely order _____ because she loves a rich, creamy, smooth, sweet cake with her tea.

A. Read the following conversations. Then tell what Tom and Laura are talking about.

1. **Tom:** I enjoy it more when it's hot. I like it with cream and sugar.
   Laura: Not me! I like it cold with lemon. _____*tea*_____

2. **Tom:** I like more ice cream than milk in mine.
   Laura: Me too. And my favorite kind is chocolate. _____

3. **Tom:** I'm thirsty! Can I taste your chocolate drink?
   Laura: Sure. It's very healthy and delicious. _____

4. **Tom:** This has lost its bubbles.
   Laura: Let me get you a cold bottle from the refrigerator._____

5. **Tom:** Yuck! I thought this juice was going to be sweet.
   Laura: I'm sorry. I gave you the wrong juice. _____

6. **Tom:** My doctor says it's healthier to drink it at
      room temperature.
   Laura: Well, I prefer it real cold! _____

B. Complete the sentences using the correct form of the **adjectives** from the box.

juicy	sweet	cold	hot

1. An orange is usually _____*juicier*_____ than an apple.

2. Cold tea is tasty, but the _____ the tea the healthier it is for you.

3. Iced coffee is _____ than freshly brewed coffee.

4. Chocolate milk is _____ than regular milk.

5. Pineapple juice is _____ than apple juice, but lemonade
   is the _____ .

6. Coffee can be served _____ or cold, but on a snowy, winter night
   the _____ the better.

C. Liquids are packaged in many containers. Write the names of two drinks from
page 35 in the **Dictionary** for each category below.

1.	can	*juice* and	
2.	carton	and	
3.	bottle	and	

A. **Vocabulary Practice**

How many words do you remember from this unit? Answer the questions using as many vocabulary words as you can without looking in the **Dictionary**. Then compare your list with another student's.

What foods do you see? List them below?

coffee

Name as many foods as you can that are not shown above.

fruits	vegetables	desserts
meats	poultry	seafood

B.

Topic: *My Favorite Restaurant and Foods*

Date: _____

What is your favorite restaurant? Where is it?
Is it in your native country? What type of food
is served there? Why is this your favorite
restaurant? Use words from this unit to
describe your favorite food.

NoTes

_____

_____

_____

_____

_____

_____

_____

Prepare your favorite food. Write the recipe below. Share your food and recipe with
the class.

INGREDIENTS:

_____   _____

_____   _____

_____   _____

INSTRUCTIONS: _____

_____

_____

_____

_____

_____

34. CITY

Dictionary pages 36–37

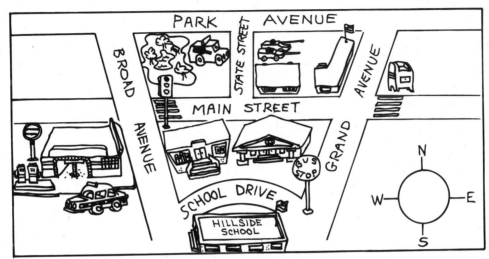

Complete the sentences using the information on the map.

A. Write *north, south, east,* or *west* to complete the conversations.

1. **Bob:** How do I get to the park?
   Sue: Walk _north_ on Broad Avenue. It's _____ of Park Avenue.

2. **Joe:** Where's the museum?
   Ann: It's _____ of Main Street.

3. **Tom:** How can I get to the Hillside School?
   Jack: Walk _____ on Grand Avenue or Broad Avenue.

4. **Paul:** I'm looking for the gas station.
   John: Drive _____ on Broad Avenue.

5. **Chris:** Where's State Street?
   Sam: It's _____ of Broad Avenue and _____ of Grand Avenue.

6. **Linda:** Where can I get ice cream?
   Steven: The truck is parked on the _____ side of State Street _____ of the park.

B. Write the words *left* or *right* to show the locations.

1. The Post Office is to the _right_ of the Police Station.
2. The taxi is parked on the _____ side of Broad Avenue.
3. The mailbox is on the _____ side of Grand Avenue.
4. The bus stop is on the _____ side of School Drive.
5. The traffic light is to the _____ of the library.

A. Read the paragraphs. Then circle the letters of the correct answers.

1. The farmer is taking the tractor out of the barn. He's going to plant a crop. He wants to prepare the field. What does he need?

   a. a brook
   (b.) a plow
   c. a bin

2. It's a beautiful summer day. Most of the animals are in the pasture. Which animal is not in the field today? (Look on pages 38 and 39 in the *Dictionary*.)

   a. a cow
   b. a sheep
   c. a horse

3. Look up! Look to your right. Then look to your left. Turn around. The trees are everywhere! There seem to be hundreds of them. Branches crackle under your feet. Where are you?

   a. in the woods
   b. on the road
   c. in the orchard

4. It's apple picking time. Get the baskets, bring the ladder, and find the children. Where are you going?

   a. to the silo
   b. to the orchard
   c. to the stream

B. Circle the word in each row that doesn't belong. Then give a reason.

1. farmhouse   barn   (horse)   silo

   A horse is not a building.

2. goat   well   stream   lake

   _____

3. chicken   sheep   cow   bridge

   _____

4. pasture   sky   grass   orchard

   _____

A. Look at the pictures. Then finish the conversations.

1. I clean the house.

B. Make sentences using words from Column A, Column B, and Column C. Use each word only once.

Column A	Column B	Column C
~~carpenter~~	repairs	numbers
accountant	writes	keys
locksmith	plants	cars
reporter	makes	flowers
mechanic	adds	stories
gardener	~~builds~~	~~walls~~

1. _A carpenter builds walls._

2. _____

3. _____

4. _____

5. _____

6. _____

C. Study the pictures on pages 40 and 41 in the **Dictionary**. Then write the occupations.

1. You want to work on a boat.

   _____sailor_____

2. You help people stay healthy.

   _____

3. You use a computer.

   _____

4. You love to draw.

   _____

5. You drive a tractor.

   _____

6. You catch fish.

   _____

7. You fix leaks.

   _____

8. You love to cook.

   _____

D. Read the following conversations. Write the first person's occupation.

1. **Juan:** How do you want it?
   Harry: Leave it long on the top, but make it short on the sides.
   Juan is a barber.

2. **Ali:** This sweater will look great on you.
   Lee: Thank you. I'll try it on.
   _____

3. **Iris:** What a perfect day to fly!
   Eva: Have a good trip.
   _____

4. **Paul:** That will be $54.00.
   Susan: I wish this medicine wasn't so expensive.
   _____

5. **Eduardo:** That long hose was just what we needed.
   Ana: You're right. I'm glad we got there in time.
   _____

6. **Carmen:** Would you like some salad with your fish?
   Paula: No, thank you. I'm not that hungry.
   _____

A. Louisa is going to buy a new dress and new shoes. Number the following items 1 to 8 to show her shopping schedule.

_____ She tries on several different dresses.

_____ She gets some money from the bank.

_____ She goes to the shoe store.

__1__ She parks her car in the parking lot.

_____ She buys shoes to match the dress.

_____ She finally buys a red dress.

_____ She goes to the department store.

_____ She gets into her car and drives home.

B. What businesses are there in your neighborhood? Check the places you usually go to.

Restaurant	
Drugstore or pharmacy	
Clothing store	
Bookstore	
Bank	
Hardware store	
Ice cream shop	
Supermarket	
Hairdresser or Barber shop	
Electronics store	

C. Look at the words below. Write the number of syllables.

__3__ **1.** bakery

_____ **2.** flower

_____ **3.** electronics

_____ **4.** jewelry

_____ **5.** clothing

_____ **6.** liquor

_____ **7.** video

_____ **8.** toy

_____ **9.** stationery

_____ **10.** supplies

D. Look at the floor plan. Complete the sentences.

1. Where is the video store?

   It's on the ___first floor___ between the ___bank___ and

   the _____ .

2. Where is the bakery?

   It's on the _____ near the _____ .

3. Where's the shoe store?

   It's on the _____ between the _____

   and the _____ .

4. Where's the music store?

   It's on the _____ near the _____ .

E. Cross out the word or words that don't belong in each sentence. Then rewrite the sentence using the correct word or words from pages 42 and 43 in the *Dictionary*.

1. I'll leave my car in the te~~lephone boot~~h.

   I'll leave my car in the parking lot.

2. You can buy a new chair in the jewelry store.

   _____

3. Let's have lunch at the toy store.

   _____

4. I'm going to get my hair cut at the bakery.

   _____

A. Look at pages 44 and 45 in the **Dictionary**. Then write the letter to complete each sentence.

_c_	**1.**	The cashier	**a.**	puts the food on the shelves.
____	**2.**	Dairy products	**b.**	uses a shopping cart or basket.
____	**3.**	The stock clerk	**c.**	uses the cash register.
____	**4.**	The fruit	**d.**	is next to the poultry.
____	**5.**	The customer	**e.**	is weighed on the scale.
____	**6.**	The fish	**f.**	include milk, cheese, and eggs.

B. Use the picture on pages 44 and 45 of the **Dictionary** to complete the chart.

Five sections of the supermarket	Foods you can find
1. Bakery	1. bread, cake
2.	2.
3.	3.
4.	4.
5.	5.

C. Look at pages 44 and 45 in the **Dictionary**. Write *is, are, isn't,* or *aren't* to complete the sentences.

1. The cashier ___is___ taking a receipt.

2. The cash register near the bakery _____ being used.

3. The customer's shopping basket _____ full.

4. The frozen food section _____ very busy.

5. A customer's shopping bag _____ on the conveyor belt.

6. The snack foods _____ near the cereals.

7. The vegetables _____ found near the fruits.

8. There _____ any animals in the supermarket.

D. Complete the crossword puzzle using words from pages 44 and 45 in the ***Dictionary***.

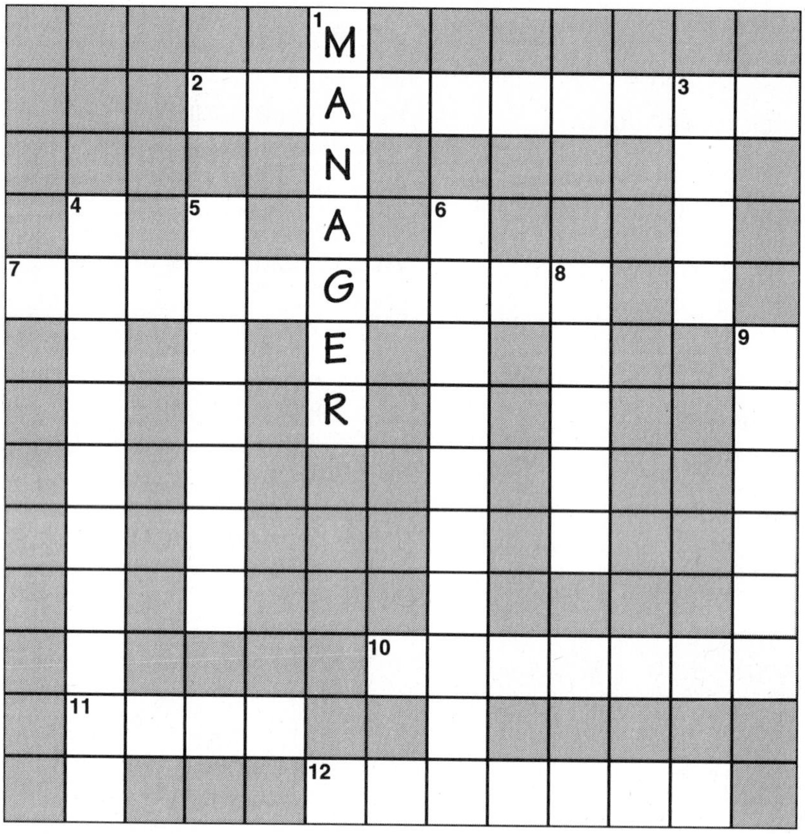

Across

2. You can find vitamins in the ______________ section. (two words)
7. ________ are used to wash clothes and dishes.
10. Chicken is found in the ________ section.
11. ________ are found near dairy products and cheese.
12. The ________ takes your money.

Down

1. The boss is called the manager.
3. The ________ counter has both meat and cheese.
4. ________ are found in the produce section.
5. The store sells many different breakfast ___________.
6. You eat __________________ between meals. (two words)
8. You use a ________ to weigh fruits and vegetables.
9. Bread comes from the ________ section.

A.   The person in each picture is having a problem. Read the words and tell what the person should buy at the drugstore.

1.   _____aspirin_____

2.   _____

3.   _____

4.   _____

5.   _____

6.   _____

B.   Look at page 46 in the ***Dictionary***. Write a letter to show where you can find each item.

   a.   on the left side of the store
   b.   in the middle of the store
   c.   on the right side of the store

   _c_   **1.**   maps

   ___   **2.**   film

   ___   **3.**   paper

   ___   **4.**   newspapers

   ___   **5.**   shaving cream

   ___   **6.**   school supplies

   ___   **7.**   magazines

   ___   **8.**   hot water bottles

   ___   **9.**   gum

   ___   **10.**   greeting cards

   ___   **11.**   flashlights

   ___   **12.**   envelopes

A. Look at page 47 in the **Dictionary**. Write the names of the items that are *on sale* in the hardware store. What else is *on sale*? Complete the chart.

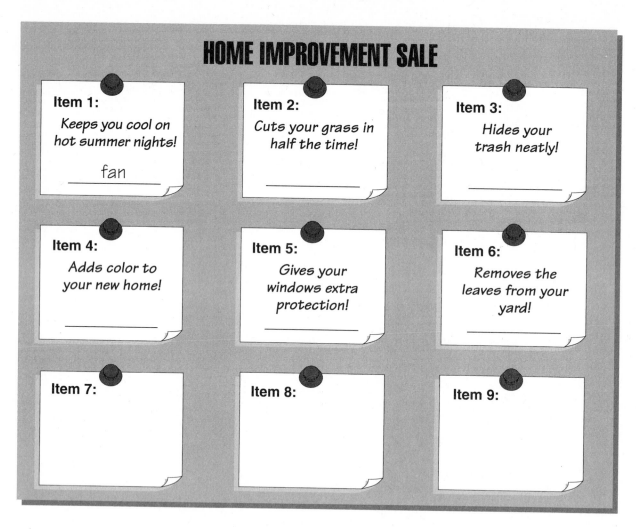

HOME IMPROVEMENT SALE

Item 1:
Keeps you cool on hot summer nights!
fan

Item 2:
Cuts your grass in half the time!

Item 3:
Hides your trash neatly!

Item 4:
Adds color to your new home!

Item 5:
Gives your windows extra protection!

Item 6:
Removes the leaves from your yard!

Item 7:

Item 8:

Item 9:

B. Tell what item each person needs. Answer in complete sentences.

1. Al wants to put some nails in the wall to hang pictures.

   He needs a hammer.

2. Carlos wants to cut some wood into small pieces.

3. Elena wants to screw a bookshelf into the wall.

4. John wants to make a lot of small, round holes in some lumber.

C. Word Search: Find ten more items that are found in the hardware store on page 47 in the **Dictionary**. Circle them. Then write them in alphabetical order.

```
G L A S S R A Z T P B
L O M H T O U G M L S
E C R O P E M B R A I
A S T V G C U R J N D
S C R E W D R I V E R
M R H L C F N C I L A
V E P K L D S K E Y S
H W I R E K O S G R J
Y S E N V U F O L M U
T G T P E G B O A R D
E X R Z L W Q P V Y Q
```

1. _____ bricks _____
2. _____
3. _____
4. _____
5. _____
6. _____
7. _____
8. _____
9. _____
10. _____
11. _____

D. Below are pictures of six problems. List all the items needed to solve each problem.

1. _____ lawn mower _____
   _____ rake _____
   _____

2. _____
   _____
   _____

3. _____
   _____
   _____

4. _____
   _____
   _____

5. _____
   _____
   _____

6. _____
   _____
   _____

A. Complete the story using words from the box.

bill	vase	menu	salad bar	candle	silverware
bar	hostess	customers	table	tablecloths	

My Favorite Restaurant

This is my favorite restaurant. I can sit at a _____table_____ for dinner, or I can
                                              1

sit at the _____ and have a drink. The _____ is very friendly.
              2   3

She shows the _____ to the tables. The place is very pretty. There is always
                  4

a _____ of flowers or a _____ on every table. The
      5   6

_____ is always shiny and the white _____ are always clean.
    7   8

There are a lot of different foods on the _____. If I only want to eat
                                              9

vegetables I can go to the _____. Best of all, the _____ is
                              10   11

never too high.

B. Make sentences using words from Column A, Column B, and Column C.

Column A	Column B	Column C
~~hostess~~	~~talks to~~	food
waitress	doesn't have	chairs
customer	leaves	stools
bar	is in	~~the customers~~
bartender	brings	liquor
silverware	pours	tip
	is on	the table

1. The hostess talks to the customers.

2. _____

3. _____

4. _____

5. _____

6. _____

A. Label the parts of the envelope and letter. Then address the package to a friend.

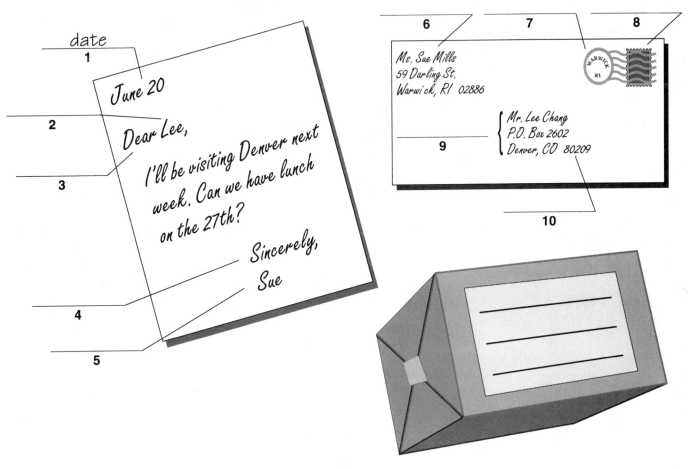

date
1

June 20

2

Dear Lee,

3

I'll be visiting Denver next week. Can we have lunch on the 27th?

Sincerely,
Sue

4

5

6   7   8

Ms. Sue Mills
59 Darling St.
Warwick, RI 02886

WARWICK
RI

Mr. Lee Chang
P.O. Box 2602
Denver, CO 80209

9

10

B. Write the letter to complete each sentence.

_d_	1. A mail carrier	**a.**	handles customers and problems in the post office.
____	2. A post card	**b.**	delivers packages overnight.
____	3. A zip code	**c.**	has the address and message on one side.
____	4. Stamps	**d.**	delivers mail directly to your home.
____	5. Express Mail	**e.**	is the center for mail activity.
____	6. A postmark	**f.**	are sold by the book or the roll.
____	7. A postal clerk	**g.**	is needed to complete the address.
____	8. A post office	**h.**	goes on top of the stamp.

A. Write *a* or *an* to complete the conversations between Ana and Bianca.

1.   **Ana:** There's __a__ typewriter near the desk.
   Bianca: I know, but it's _____ old typewriter.

2.   **Ana:** Do you want _____ cup of coffee?
   Bianca: Yes, please. I left _____ orange cup near the coffee maker.

3.   **Ana:** Complete the form and mail _____ check to the doctor.
   Bianca: O.K. I'll need _____ typewriter, _____ envelope, and _____ stamp.

4.   **Ana:** Please organize the papers on my desk.
   Bianca: Sure. I'll need ___ pen, ___ in-box, and ___ out-box.

5.   **Ana:** Here's your office. It has _____ new desk, _____ chair, and _____ new computer. What else will you need?
   Bianca: I'll need _____ dictionary, ___ stapler, ___ pencil sharpener, ___ tape dispenser, and _____ appointment book.

B. Which of these machines have you used? Check (✔) *Yes* or *No* column. After each *Yes*, tell where you used it.

Machine	Yes	No	Where used
Computer	✔		at the public library
Typewriter			
Switchboard			
Stapler			
Coffee machine			
Pencil sharpener			
Photocopier			
Telephone			
Printer			
Water fountain			

A. Look at the picture on page 51 in the **Dictionary**. Then fill in the blanks.

1. You get one every month.   *monthly statement*

2. You need it to operate the cash machine.   _____

3. You can use it if you don't want to leave your car.   _____

4. This person helps you borrow money from a bank.   _____

5. You keep them in a checkbook.   _____

6. The bank officer takes them out of the vault.   _____

7. You buy them before taking a long trip.   _____

8. It tells you how much money you have saved.   _____

9. You use this to put money in the bank.   _____

10. This card lets you charge now and pay later.   _____

B. Answer the questions using complete sentences.

1. Where are the safety deposit boxes in a bank?

   They are in the bank vault.

2. What piece of paper do you need to deposit money in the bank?

   _____

   _____

3. Who works in a bank but doesn't handle money?

   _____

   _____

4. What other card looks almost like a credit card?

   _____

   _____

C. Cross out the word or words that don't belong. Then rewrite the sentences using the correct word or words from page 51 in the *Dictionary*.

1. You need a ~~coin~~ to operate the automatic teller machine.

   You need an ATM card to operate an automatic teller machine.

2. The checks are kept in the bank vault.

   _____

3. A bank officer usually works at the drive-through window.

   _____

4. A withdrawal slip is one kind of identification.

   _____

5. The security guard works at a big desk.

   _____

D. Read each of the sentences. Then write a short sentence telling what each person should do.

1. I only have bills. I can't use them to take the bus.

   Ask for some change.

2. I don't want to lose these important papers.

   _____

3. I need to cash a check, but I don't want to get out of my car.

   _____

4. I don't know how much money I have in my savings account.

   _____

5. I need to get $100 cash out of my savings account.

   _____

68

A. Study the two pictures. Write five sentences telling about the differences between the two classrooms.

Classroom A   **Classroom B**

1. There is no chalk in Classroom B. _____

2. _____

3. _____

4. _____

5. _____

B. Here are some ways of doing well in school. Number the sentences 1 to 6 to show what you would do after you read all the assignments.

_____ Make notes in your notebook every day.

_____ Ask questions at the end of the class if you don't understand.

Read all assignments.

_____ Listen carefully for the teacher to give information.

_____ Check to see that all the homework is complete.

_____ Find a quiet place at home to study.

_____ Take your textbook home every night.

C. Pedro is writing a note to his friend. Complete the note using words from pages 52 and 53 in the **Dictionary**.

Dear Luis,

Life is very different here at Mercer _college_ 1. The _____ 2 is beautiful. There are lots of trees and flowers. I sleep in a _____ 3 but I study in the _____ 4 because it's quiet there. I meet my friends at the _____ 5. The _____ 6 are not like our high school teachers. They expect us to work much harder. I had a _____ 7 Monday and my _____ 8 was not so good. Sometimes I wonder if I will ever get to _____ 9 and receive my _____ 10. Why am I so worried? I've only been here three days!

Sincerely,

Pedro

D. Write a letter to complete each sentence.

_c_ **1.** The registrar   **a.** is used on a blackboard.

____ **2.** Graduation   **b.** is a college teacher.

____ **3.** A dormitory   **c.** can give you a transcript.

____ **4.** Chalk   **d.** holds coats and hats.

____ **5.** A principal   **e.** supervises many teachers.

____ **6.** A professor   **f.** is where students sleep.

____ **7.** A locker   **g.** is the same as a score.

____ **8.** A grade   **h.** is the same as commencement.

A. Circle the letters of the words that complete the relationships.

1.	boat: wading pool	shovel:	a. seesaw **(b.)** sandbox c. bench d. slide
2.	bicycle: two	tricycle:	a. one b. two c. three d. four
3.	bench: sit	jungle gym:	a. climb b. see c. sit d. walk
4.	jump rope: three	seesaw:	a. one b. two c. three d. four
5.	sand: sandbox	water:	a. kite b. hopscotch c. wading pool d. jungle gym

B. Read the conversations. Then tell what the children are talking about.

1. **Girl:** I like to climb up slowly and come down fast.
   Boy: I like to close my eyes.
   They're talking about using the slide.

2. **Girl:** Don't throw that stuff around.
   Boy: I'm sorry. Did any get in your eyes?
   _____

3. **Girl:** Look how high up it is!
   Boy: That's because it's a windy day.
   _____

4. **Girl:** He stepped on a line.
   Boy: I know. It's difficult to hop on one foot.
   _____

5. **Girl:** There must be eleven people on this thing.
   Boy: That's why I like it so much.
   _____

A. Read the questions. Circle the letters of the correct answers.

1. Alex doesn't have any homework to do. He has an hour before his next class. He wants to read the latest news. Where should he go?
   a. to the microfilm reader
   b. to the periodicals section
   c. to the encyclopedia

2. Boun Ome doesn't know where to find the books on electricity. Where should he start?
   a. at the book return
   b. at the audio-visual section
   c. at the card catalog

3. Which line on the file card tells what the book is about?
   a. title
   b. author
   c. subject

4. Name one place you can't find music.
   a. the periodicals section
   b. the tapes section
   c. the records section

B. Look at page 55 in the **Dictionary**. Name each item pictured below. Then tell what it's near.

1. _____a globe_____   The globe is near the encyclopedias. _____

2. _____   _____

3. _____   _____

4. _____   _____

5. _____   _____

A. Look at the pictures on pages 56 and 57 in the *Dictionary*. Then match each item in Column A with an item in Column B.

Column A

   f   **1.** witness stand

_____ **2.** transcript

_____ **3.** gun holster

_____ **4.** robe

_____ **5.** parking ticket

_____ **6.** nightstick

_____ **7.** defense attorney

_____ **8.** jail cell

Column B

a. traffic cop

b. judge

c. police officer

d. defendant

e. meter maid

f. witness

g. court reporter

h. suspect

B. Look at the pictures on page 56 and 57 in the *Dictionary*.

1. List four people who work for the police department.

   police officer   _____

_____   _____

2. Name three things that police officers carry or wear.

_____   _____   _____

3. Name five people who are in the courtroom.

_____   _____   _____

_____   _____

4. Look at the courtroom picture again. Name three pieces of furniture in the room.

_____   _____   _____

5. What do you think the lawyer is saying?

_____

_____

C. Complete the crossword puzzle using the courtroom words on page 57 in the **Dictionary**.

		¹R	E	P	O	²R	T	E	R				³	
⁴										⁵				
							⁶							
⁷			⁸											
												⁹		
	¹⁰					¹¹								
¹²														
				¹³										

Across

1. The court __reporter__ writes down every word that is said in the courtroom.
4. The defense attorney helps the _____.
5. There are twelve people in the _____.
7. The witness must sit in the _____ _____.
11. A _____ cop directs cars on a busy street.
12. Only the judge wears a _____.
13. If you witness an _____ you may have to tell the jury what you saw.

Down

2. The court reporter writes out a _____.
3. A person who guards prisoners is a _____.
5. A _____ sits behind the bench in court.
6. Another word for attorney is _____.
8. The jury must look carefully at the _____.
9. The police give a _____ for speeding.
10. The room where the judge, jury, and witnesses meet is called the _____.

74

A. Finish numbering the following items to 8 to show how the fire department responded to a fire.

_____ The fire fighters attached hoses to the hydrant.

_____ The smoke detector made a loud sound.

_____ The fire truck went to Bill's house.

_1_ A fire started in Bill's house.

_____ The fire fighters put on their coats and helmets.

_____ The fire fighters used fire hoses to put out the fire.

_____ Bill called the fire station.

_____ The fire fighters heard the fire alarm.

B. Make sentences using words from Column A, Column B, and Column C.

Column A	Column B	Column C
~~fire hydrant~~	makes	sick people
fire extinguisher	can break	loud noise
siren	~~provides~~	window
ax	helps	fire
paramedic	protects	~~water~~
helmet	can stop	head

1. A fire hydrant provides water. _____

2. _____

3. _____

4. _____

5. _____

6. _____

C. Answer these questions using complete sentences.

1. Why do the fire fighters use a fire pole?

_____

2. What does a bull horn do?

_____

A. Write the name of the ailment next to each picture. Then match each illness with one of the suggestions.

1. ___c___  ___toothache___   **a.** See a doctor.

2. _____  _____   **b.** Take an aspirin.

3. _____  _____   **c.** See a dentist.

4. _____  _____   **d.** Don't eat anything else.

5. _____  _____   **e.** Put a bandage on it.

B. Which ailments have you had recently? What did you do about them? Complete the chart below.

Ailment or Illness	When I had it	What I did about it
headache		
backache		
sunburn		
toothache		
blister		
cold		

51.   DENTAL

A.   Write **T** for True or **F** for False.

___T___   **1.**   The oral hygienist helps the dentist.

_____   **2.**   Dental floss is used to clean between the teeth.

_____   **3.**   A cavity is a hole in a tooth.

_____   **4.**   The dentist gives anesthetic after he fills a tooth.

_____   **5.**   The patient uses the mirror.

_____   **6.**   X-rays can show the inside of a tooth.

_____   **7.**   Dentures are the same as false teeth.

_____   **8.**   The dentist sits in the dentist chair.

_____   **9.**   A drill is used to make a hole in a tooth.

_____   **10.**   Plaque and tartar cause cavities.

B.   Circle the word in each row that doesn't belong. Then give a reason for your choice.

1.   (dentures)   dentist   patient   oral hygienist

   *The other words describe people, not things.*_____

2.   toothbrush   toothpaste   dental floss   x-ray

   _____

3.   plaque   tartar   dentist chair   cavity

   _____

4.   drill   toothpaste   filling   anesthetic

   _____

C.   Complete the following chart.

	How often I do it	How often I should do it
brush my teeth		
floss my teeth		
see the dentist		

A. Look at the pictures on pages 62 and 63 in the **Dictionary**. Write **a**, **b**, or **c** to show where you can find each item most of the time.

      a. in the emergency room

      b. in the hospital room

      c. in the operating room

_c_ **1.** monitor   ____ **7.** patient's chart

____ **2.** surgeon   ____ **8.** x-rays

____ **3.** cotton balls   ____ **9.** intravenous

____ **4.** gurney   ____ **10.** physical therapist

____ **5.** alcohol   ____ **11.** cast

____ **6.** anesthesiologist   ____ **12.** flowers

B. Look at the pictures on pages 62 and 63 in the **Dictionary**. Write *is*, *are*, *isn't*, or *aren't* to complete the sentences.

1. There ___aren't___ any cotton balls in the hospital room.

2. The patient _____ very happy.

3. There _____ a lot of instruments in the operating room.

4. There _____ a lot of people at the admitting desk.

5. There _____ one surgeon in the operating room.

6. A young girl _____ sitting on the examination table.

7. The surgical nurses _____ wearing masks.

8. The surgery _____ finished.

9. Why _____ there a wheel chair in the hospital room?

10. _____ the doctor using a stethoscope?

C. Write the name of the item next to each picture. Then match each item with the description.

1. __d__   __cast__   **a.** It cleans the skin.

2. _____   _____   **b.** It's like a bed that has wheels.

3. _____   _____   **c.** You need a prescription to get it.

4. _____   _____   **d.** It's for a broken leg.

5. _____   _____   **e.** They're used to examine the mouth.

6. _____   _____   **f.** A surgeon uses them.

7. _____   _____   **g.** It's used for patients who can't walk.

A.   Use one of the following contractions to help describe each person or branch of the U.S. Government.

it's	they're	he's/she's

1.   **Congress:** ___It's___ the branch of the government that makes the laws. _____ made up of the House of Representatives and the Senate.

2.   **President:** _____ the elected leader of the country.

3.   **Justices of the Supreme Court:** _____ people who approve the laws. They can tell Congress to change the laws if they go against the Constitution.

4.   **Declaration of Independence:** _____ an important document that says that "all men are created equal."

5.   **Senate:** _____ the part of Congress with two senators from each state.

6.   **Members of Congress:** _____ people elected to serve in Congress.

B.   Write the following words in alphabetical order.

President Senate	White House House of Representatives	Congress Justices	U. S. Capitol Building Constitution

1.   ___Congress___

2.   _____

3.   _____

4.   _____

5.   _____

6.   _____

7.   _____

8.   _____

C.   Answer these questions about your native country.

1.   Do you have a President?   Yes _____   No _____

2.   If you do have a President, what is his or her name? _____

3.   If you don't have a President, who leads the country? _____

4.   What is the highest court in your country called? _____

A. **Vocabulary Practice**

How many words do you remember from this unit? Answer the questions using as many vocabulary words as you can without looking in the **Dictionary**. Then compare your list with another student's.

Who are these people? Where do they work? List their occupations and the stores or buildings they work in. Add the names, professions, and occupations of other people who work in your community.

Complete the floor plan of the shopping center with the names of stores that are in your community.

My Shopping Center

Occupation	Store/Building
teacher	school

Now make a list of all the vocabulary words you can think of to answer these questions.

What can you buy in a hardware store, supermarket, drugstore?

What can you find in a library?

Why would you visit the doctor or a hospital?

What is needed to put out a fire?

B. Notes to Myself

Topic: *My Community*

Date: _____

Do you live in the city or the country?
What does your community look like?
Include words from this unit to help
describe your neighborhood.

_____

_____

_____

_____

_____

_____

_____

Have any of the following events ever happened to you?
Describe one of your experiences.

1.   Witnessing or being in an automobile accident
2.   Witnessing or being in a fire
3.   Witnessing a bank robbery
4.   Graduating high school, the university, or college
5.   Visiting or staying in a hospital

_____

_____

_____

_____

_____

_____

55. PETS AND FARM

Dictionary pages 65–67

A. Work with a partner to complete each category of animals on the following chart.

Dogs		Rodents	
1.	mutt	1.	
2.		2.	
3.		3.	
4.		4.	
5.			

Birds		Fish	
1.		1.	
2.		2.	
3.			

B. Choose two animals you might like to have as pets. Explain why. Then choose two animals you wouldn't like to have as pets and explain why.

PETS I WOULD LIKE TO HAVE

parrot

I like to hear parrots talk.

1. _____

2. _____

PETS I WOULDN'T LIKE TO HAVE

1. _____

2. _____

C. Read the conversations. Tell what animals and farm items Rosa and Luis are talking about.

1. **Rosa:** Wow, look how round and fat they are!
   Luis: I see. And rolling in the mud makes them feel good!

   They're talking about the pigs.

2. **Rosa:** What's that black and white animal over there?
   Luis: Don't scare it. It makes a terrible smell!

3. **Rosa:** Where do they keep hay for the animals?
   Luis: Up there, where the pitchfork is.

4. **Rosa:** Isn't that a cute little animal!
   Luis: It sure is. And it lays lots of eggs!

5. **Rosa:** It looks like a horse.
   Luis: Yes, but its ears are a lot longer.

D. Check the boxes to show what each animal can do.

	run/trot	fly	give milk	carry people on its back
cow			✔	
chicken				
horse				
rooster				
colt				
duck				
goat				
donkey				

A. Study the pictures on pages 68 and 69 in the *Dictionary*. Then fill in the blanks.

1. It has a white face with black around the eyes. _____panda_____

2. It's the only animal with a trunk. _____

3. It carries its baby in a pouch. _____

4. It can pull its head and legs under its shell. _____

5. This bird has a very large and beautiful tail. _____

6. It's all white and loves fish. _____

7. It looks like a big, gray dog. _____

8. This animal has long legs and a long neck. _____

9. This animal can carry a lot of water. _____

10. This animal has stripes on its tail, but they're not black and white. _____

B. Answer the questions using complete sentences.

What is the difference between:

1. a snake and a lizard?

   A lizard has legs, but a snake doesn't.

2. a giraffe and a zebra?

   _____

3. a monkey and a gorilla?

   _____

4. a deer and a llama?

   _____

C. Pedro felt lazy. He didn't want to play with anyone. He walked through the corn field behind his house and lay down on a pile of hay. He closed his eyes. Soon he was fast asleep! Finish Pedro's dream.

The sky was getting dark at the Town Zoo. Children were everywhere.
The animals were making a lot of noise. Something was scaring them.
The gorillas were

_____

_____

_____

_____

D. Do you ever dream? Can you remember one of your dreams? Share it with a friend.

_____

_____

_____

A. Look at the birds on page 70 in the **Dictionary.** Then answer the questions using complete sentences.

1. Which bird is completely pink?

   The flamingo is completely pink.

2. Which one makes holes in trees?

3. Which one lays blue eggs?

4. Which one has two very long tail feathers?

5. Which one is completely blue?

6. Which one can't fly?

7. Which one has a very long bill?

8. Which one is completely white?

9. Which one often stands on one leg?

10. Your turn to ask a question.

B. Answer the questions using the birds' names on page 70 in the **Dictionary.**

1. Which birds live in your native country?

2. Which birds have you seen in a zoo?

C. Make up a true sentence about each bird using words from Column A, Column B, and Column C.

Column A	Column B	Column C
~~crane~~	has	crow
robin	eats	blue eggs
blackbird	~~lives~~	orange and green feathers
pelican	looks like	fish
flamingo	lays	~~water~~
mallard		long neck

1. The crane always lives near water. _____

2. _____

3. _____

4. _____

5. _____

6. _____

D. Look at the birds on page 70 of the *Dictionary*. Complete each sentence using the correct comparative **adjective**. Write *longer* or *shorter*, *bigger* or *smaller*.

1. A flamingo's neck is ___longer___ than a crane's neck.

2. A stork's bill is _____ than a pelican's bill.

3. A pigeon is _____ than a hummingbird.

4. A cardinal is _____ than a bluebird.

5. A sparrow's tail is _____ than a cardinal's tail.

6. A flamingo's legs are _____ than a stork's legs.

7. A sparrow's feet are _____ than a crow's feet.

8. A hummingbird's feathers are _____ than a vulture's feathers.

Compare two birds. Use the same **adjectives** as above.

9. _____

10. _____

A. Study the pictures of the fish. Write sentences describing the differences.

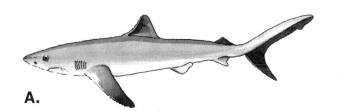

A.

B.

1. Fish A has big fins, but Fish B has small fins. _____

2. _____

3. _____

4. _____

B. Look at the pictures on page 71 in the **Dictionary**. Then read the signs on the fish tanks. Tell what fish or sea animal lives in each tank.

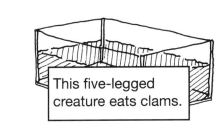

This five-legged creature eats clams.

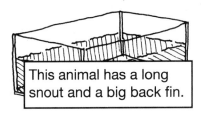

This animal has a long snout and a big back fin.

1. _____ starfish _____

2. _____

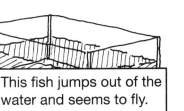

This fish jumps out of the water and seems to fly.

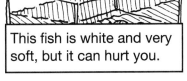

This fish is white and very soft, but it can hurt you.

3. _____

4. _____

C. Write **a**, **b**, or **c** to help describe the fish and sea mammals. You can use more than one letter for each item.

a. is harmful
b. is eaten
c. is not a fish

_b_	**1.** herring		____	**7.** starfish
____	**2.** eel		____	**8.** shark
____	**3.** jellyfish		____	**9.** bass
____	**4.** octopus		____	**10.** perch
____	**5.** whitefish		____	**11.** barracuda
____	**6.** trout		____	**12.** squid

D. Have you eaten any of these fish or sea animals? Check *Yes* or *No*. After each *Yes* tell where you ate it. Then tell if you liked it or not.

	Yes	No	Where	Did you like it?
catfish	X		In my native country	Yes
squid				
herring				
bass				
shark				
octopus				
whitefish				
perch				
hake				
sailfish				

A.   Look at the pictures on page 72 in the **Dictionary**.

1.   Which insects can't fly?

_____ant_____   _____   _____

_____   _____   _____

2.   Which insects often bite people?

_____   _____   _____

3.   Which insects are green?

_____   _____   _____

4.   Which insects have many beautiful colors on their wings?

_____   _____   _____

B.   Circle the letters of the words that complete the relationships.

1. bee : hive	ant :	a. cocoon (b.) anthill c. wasp d. hive
2. baby bird : egg	butterfly :	a. anthill b. termite c. bee d. cocoon
3. green : praying mantis	red :	a. ladybug b. caterpillar c. flea d. cicada
4. locust : cricket	bee :	a. hive b. wasp c. spider d. centipede
5. light : firefly	sting :	a. moth b. caterpillar c. scorpion d. cocoon
6. spider : web	capterpillar :	a. hive b. cocoon c. anthill d. moth

C. Complete the story using words from the box.

ants	walking stick	cocoon	caterpillar	bee	spider
wasp		butterfly	scorpion	web	praying mantis

Insects have unusual lives. The _caterpillar_ makes a _____ for itself.
                                                1   2

After sleeping in it for several months, the caterpillar comes out as a brightly colored

_____.
    3

_____ and _____ come out of eggs. The spider must build a
      4   5

_____ to catch its food. When other insects fall into this trap they are eaten.
    6

Two insects that can fly and sting are the _____ and the _____.
                                                7   8
The _____ can't fly, but its sting can kill a person.
    9

Some animals try to look like plants. The _____ looks like a twig from a
                                          10

tree, and the _____ looks almost like a leaf.
             11

D. Write a letter or letters to complete each sentence.

_a, c, e_   **1.** A mouse   **a.** has pink ears.

_____   **2.** A chipmunk   **b.** often climbs trees.

_____   **3.** A squirrel   **c.** is smaller than a chipmunk.

_____   **4.** A rat   **d.** can't run very fast.

_____   **5.** A gopher   **e.** has a long, thin tail.

                                    f. has a white stripe on its side.

                                    g. looks like a big mouse.

                                    h. is larger than a squirrel.

                                    i. has a bushy tail.

A. Read the questions. Circle the letters of the correct answer.

1. Jai Soon wants to plant a tree that will be green all year long. Which tree should he plant?
   - **a.** a pine
   - **b.** a maple
   - **c.** a magnolia

2. Mika saw a tree with white bark in the park. What kind of tree did she see?
   - **a.** a eucalyptus
   - **b.** a redwood
   - **c.** a birch

3. Chang likes seeing the trees change colors in the autumn. What kind of tree is he looking at?
   - **a.** cactus
   - **b.** palm
   - **c.** maple

4. Rita uses plants to give flavor to her cooking. What kind of plants does she use?
   - **a.** weeds
   - **b.** herbs
   - **c.** house plants

B. Circle the word in each row that doesn't belong. Give a reason for your choice.

1. weed   branch   twig   leaf

   A weed isn't part of a tree.

2. pine   birch   willow   vine

3. house plant   fern   herbs   oak

4. eucalyptus   bush   elm   redwood

5. needle   cone   trunk   fern

A. Complete the crossword puzzle by using the plural form of the names of the flowers and their parts from page 74 of the **Dictionary**. Add *s*, *es*, or *ies* to form the plural.

		¹F		²			³								
		L													
⁴		O						⁵	⁶			⁷		⁸	
		W													
		E		⁹											
	¹⁰	R													
		S													
	¹¹														

Across

2. _____ are small bunches of flowers worn by a women on their waists or shoulders.

4. _____ are found on the stems of roses.

5. _____ are rings of flowers and leaves.

10. Nurseries are also called _____.

11. _____ have white petals and yellow centers.

Down

1. Flowers _____ are plants that bloom.

3. _____ are daisy-like flowers with yellow petals.

6. _____ are flowers that have thorns.

7. _____ are plants that have long leaves and cup-shaped flowers.

8. _____ are the main support of flowers and plants.

9. _____ are leaf-like parts of flowers.

A.   **Vocabulary Practice**

How many words do you remember from this unit? Answer the questions using as many vocabulary words as you can without looking in the **Dictionary**. Then compare your list with another student's.

List the parts of the tree, the plants, the insects, and the rodents you see in the picture below. Then add to your list all the other names of the trees, plants, insects, and rodents you can remember.

What flowers are grown in this greenhouse? List them.

orchid

trunk

You're going to the zoo. Name all the animals you might see there. Circle the names of those animals you might have as a pet.

(turtle)
elephant

B. Notes to Myself

Notes

Topic: *My Experience with Nature*

Date: _____

Have you ever been to a zoo, a farm, an aquarium, or a bird sanctuary? Use the animal and farm words in this unit to help you describe your experience.

_____

_____

_____

_____

_____

_____

_____

Do you have a pet or a favorite animal? Do you have a garden or a favorite flower? Write a short paragraph telling about *your favorite* thing in nature.

_____

_____

_____

_____

_____

_____

63. AIRPORT/AIRPLANE

Dictionary pages 75-77

A. Complete the conversation between Ana and Marcos using pages 75 and 76 in the **Dictionary** and the information on the airport schedule.

LADO INTERNATIONAL AIRPORT

ARRIVALS

	GATE	DEPARTED	DUE	ARRIVED
BOSTON	8	1:30	2:30	2:30
DALLAS	12	2:00	5:00	4:45
DALLAS	4	2:30	5:30	5:30
MIAMI	3	2:00	5:30	canceled
SEATTLE	9	9:30	1:30	1:30

Ana: I'm tired of waiting in the ___*airport*___ for Dad's _____ from
                                         1   **2**
Dallas. We've been standing in this _____ _____ too long!
                                              3

Marcos: Dad said he would be on the two o'clock plane from Dallas. Let's go look

at the _____ _____. Didn't he tell us to wait at Gate ___?
              4   **5**

Ana: Yes, he did. And it's after five o'clock. Maybe he missed the plane.

Marcos: Look! There's a later plane coming in from Dallas.

Ana: Let's go to Gate ___ and wait for him there.
                         6

Marcos: We'd better hurry. We don't have much time.

Ana: Wow! This airport is so busy! Dad always said to keep your _____ in
                                                                            7
your pocket and carry your own _____ when the
                                    8
airport is this crowded.

Marcos: Hurry up, Ana! Let's go find Grandpa!

B. Look at the airport schedule above. Write **T** for True or **F** for False.

___T___ **1.** Most of the planes arrived on time.

_____ **2.** The flight from Seattle is shorter than the flight from Boston.

_____ **3.** The flight from Miami arrived early.

_____ **4.** The first plane from Dallas came in on time.

_____ **5.** The flight from Seattle arrived at Gate 9.

_____ **6.** The arrival gates for the flights from Boston and Seattle are near each other.

_____ **7.** The flight from Boston left early in the morning.

_____ **8.** Both flights from Dallas took the same time.

C. Study the pictures on pages 76 and 77 in the **Dictionary**. Then match each item in Column A with an item in Column B.

Column A	Column B
_c_ **1.** ticket agent	**a.** sits next to the captain
____ **2.** porter	**b.** flies the plane
____ **3.** security guard	**c.** sells tickets
____ **4.** passenger	**d.** assists the pilot
____ **5.** captain	**e.** protects passengers
____ **6.** co-pilot	**f.** gets an aisle seat or a window seat
____ **7.** navigator	**g.** serves food to the passengers
____ **8.** flight attendant	**h.** carries luggage for passengers

D. You're planning an airplane trip. Number the following items 1 to 10 to help you organize your trip.

____ Give your luggage to a sky cap at the terminal building.

____ Buy your plane ticket several weeks before the trip.

____ Get on the plane.

_1_ Find your passport and get a visa.

____ Go to the waiting area.

____ Go through the metal detector.

____ Enjoy the trip!

____ Go to the airport.

____ Check in at the ticket counter.

____ Fasten your seat belt.

E. Look at the list in exercise **D**. What other things have you done when you've traveled by plane?

_____

_____

98

F. Look at pages 76 and 77 in the *Dictionary*. Answer the questions using two complete sentences.

1. Is the movie in the cabin about animals?

   No, it isn't. The movie is about a man and a woman.

2. Is the sky cap sitting at the ticket counter?

3. Is the flight attendant sitting in first class?

4. Is the security guard on the airplane?

5. Is the man with earphones sitting in economy class?

6. Are all the passengers sitting near the window?

G. Look at pages 76 and 77 in the *Dictionary*. Complete the sentences using the *past tense* of the **verbs** in parentheses.

1. The passengers __watched__ the movie. *(watch)*
2. The captain _____ the plane. *(fly)*
3. The man in first class _____ a seat belt. *(wear)*
4. The passenger _____ through the metal detector. *(walk)*
5. The porter _____ the suitcases. *(push)*
6. Many passengers _____ in economy class. *(sit)*
7. The cars were _____ in the garage. *(park)*
8. The Air Tram van _____ for the passengers. *(wait)*
9. Some passengers _____ juice on the plane. *(drink)*
10. The co-pilot _____ a lot of clouds. *(see)*

H. Have you ever been on an airplane? Explain how it feels.

A. Read the classified ads. Look at page 78 in the **Dictionary** to decide what item is being advertised. Then write two of your own ads for transportation.

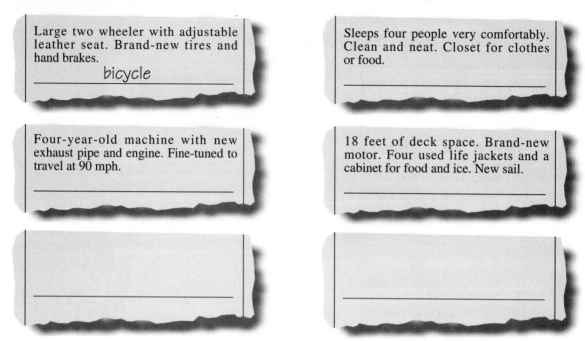

Large two wheeler with adjustable leather seat. Brand-new tires and hand brakes.

bicycle

Sleeps four people very comfortably. Clean and neat. Closet for clothes or food.

_____

Four-year-old machine with new exhaust pipe and engine. Fine-tuned to travel at 90 mph.

_____

18 feet of deck space. Brand-new motor. Four used life jackets and a cabinet for food and ice. New sail.

_____

B. Complete the sentences using the **comparative adjectives** from the box.

bigger	smaller	slower	faster
biggest	smallest	slowest	fastest

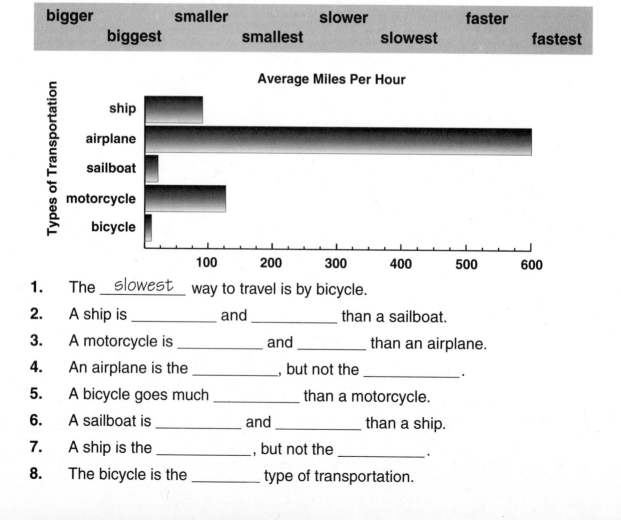

Average Miles Per Hour

Types of Transportation: ship, airplane, sailboat, motorcycle, bicycle

100   200   300   400   500   600

1. The ___*slowest*___ way to travel is by bicycle.

2. A ship is _____ and _____ than a sailboat.

3. A motorcycle is _____ and _____ than an airplane.

4. An airplane is the _____, but not the _____.

5. A bicycle goes much _____ than a motorcycle.

6. A sailboat is _____ and _____ than a ship.

7. A ship is the _____, but not the _____.

8. The bicycle is the _____ type of transportation.

A. Louisa has been having car trouble. She and Rosa are talking about buying new cars. Complete the conversation using words from pages 79 and 80 in the **Dictionary.**

Rosa: So, what kind of car are you going to buy?

Louisa: I love small cars, but a _____compact_____ is just too small.
                                           1

Rosa: If you love fresh air you could buy a _____ .
                                                          2

Louisa: Oh no. My hair would always be a mess. Anyway, I need a big car to take

my son's soccer team to out-of-town games. So I was thinking about a

_____ or a _____ .
         3   4

Rosa: Well, if I know you, you'll probably buy a plain, old _____ .
                                                                           5

Louisa: You're right. But it has to have an _____ transmission. I can't drive
                                                          6

a manual transmission. And I don't like to be hot in the summer so I must

have an _____ .
               7

Rosa: And of course you will want to listen to music as you drive, so you will also

need a _____ .
              8

Louisa: Actually, I'll be happy with any new car. I'm tired of having a _____
                                                                                       9

come so often to take my car in for repairs.

B. Complete the lists below using words from page 80 in the **Dictionary**.

Things that make a car safer		Things that make a car more comfortable
1. horn		1.
2.		2.
3.		3.
4.		4.
5.		

Instruments that measure things in a car
1.
2.
3.

C. Below are pictures of five car problems. For each picture, list any items on pages 79 and 80 in the **Dictionary** that could solve each problem.

1. _____ spare tire, jack _____

2. _____

3. _____

4. _____

5. _____

D. Word Search: Find ten items that are found in a car. Use words from page 80 in the **Dictionary**. Circle them. List the words below.

S	T	I	C	K	S	H	I	F	T
P	X	A	G	S	M	O	T	O	R
E	O	H	F	A	Z	R	O	M	T
E	R	O	B	Q	I	N	B	E	N
D	A	S	H	B	O	A	R	D	E
O	D	E	M	I	D	J	A	N	P
M	I	C	H	V	A	C	K	T	U
E	O	M	B	A	T	T	E	R	Y
T	G	F	A	N	B	E	L	T	A
E	B	O	C	L	N	V	M	U	Z
R	A	D	I	A	T	O	R	G	N

1. _____ speedometer _____

2. _____

3. _____

4. _____

5. _____

6. _____

7. _____

8. _____

9. _____

10. _____

A. Read the following conversations. What types of transportation are the people using?

1. **Tom:** Are we going to stop at Jones Road?
   Ann: I don't know. I'll ask the conductor.

   They're on a train.
   _____

2. **Luis:** What's the fare?
   Marra: The meter shows $5.50.

   _____

3. **Young Su:** I want to get off at the next corner.
   Soo Mi: Just pull the cord and the driver will stop.

   _____

4. **Carlos:** Oh, there's the station entrance.
   Helena: You're right. Let's get tokens for the turnstile.

   _____

5. **Mario:** It feels like we're on a train.
   Marta: Yes, but there's only one car. Hold on to the pole so you don't fall off.

   _____

B. Complete the chart by checking the correct column.

	Train	Subway	Taxi	Bus	Trolley
Uses tracks	X	X			X
Uses tickets					
Uses platforms					
Uses a schedule					
Has a meter					
Has a conductor					
Goes anywhere					
Uses tokens					
Has turnstiles					
Stops at street corners					

C. Read the conversation between Maria and Pablo. Complete the train schedule by writing in the air fares.

DESTINATION	ROUND-TRIP FARES	
	Regular	Discount
New York		
Miami		
Boston	$89	
Montreal		

Pablo: Maria, look at this ad in the newspaper.

Maria: What's it about, Pablo?

Pablo: Discount train fares.

Maria: You mean if we want to visit Grandpa in Boston we don't have to pay as much as we did last year?

Pablo: Well, see for yourself!

Maria: Wow! Last year we each paid $89 to take the train to Boston. Now we can get tickets for $58.

Pablo: And we only have to pay $63 to visit Aunt Tina in Miami.

Maria: Last year it cost us each $95.

Pablo: Hey, now you can visit your friend Marta in New York. Those tickets aren't going to go any lower than $35. Maria, that's half the price of a regular ticket.

Maria: We should tell Mom and Dad about this. I'll bet they'd think about a short vacation if they knew it would only cost the two of them $100 to go to Montreal.

Pablo: That trip cost them twice that price last summer.

Maria: I know! Let's go find Mom and Dad.

A. Write the correct **verbs** in the box. Then include a few rules of your own.

speed	cross	drive	
stop		pass	slow

RULES OF THE ROAD

Do	**Don't**
1. <u>slow</u> down at an exit.	1. _____ over a solid line.
2. _____ at a stop sign.	2. _____ through a caution light.
3. _____ on the right.	3. _____ through a red light.
4. _____ down near a toll booth.	4. _____ in a No Passing Zone.
5. _____ slower in the right lane.	5. _____ up at a pedestrian crossing.
6. _____ at a railroad crossing.	6. _____ down in the left lane.
7. _____.	7. _____.
8. _____.	8. _____.

B. Look at each pair of signs below. Explain the difference between the two signs.

1. <u>You don't have to stop completely for a yield sign.</u>

2. _____

3. _____

4. _____

105

C. Draw pictures of road signs in the spaces below.

1. Be careful. There's a railroad crossing ahead.

2. You can't pass another car on this part of the road.

3. You can only turn left here.

4. Don't go faster than 35 miles per hour.

5. Children may be crossing the road ahead.

6. Don't make a U turn on this street.

D. Complete the sentences using **conjunctions** from the box.

and	but	because	or

1. Stop at the stop sign ___*or*___ you might get into an accident.

2. Pass carefully on the left, _____ look before you go.

3. Go over the railroad tracks slowly _____ a train could be coming.

4. You could get off at this exit, _____ you could get off at that exit.

5. Take out your money _____ slow down when you get to a toll booth.

6. You could try to drive down a one-way street, _____ you will probably get a ticket.

7. When you're in a hurry, drive in the left lane _____ the cars go faster there.

8. Slow down in the school zone _____ let the children cross.

A. **Vocabulary Practice**

How many words do you remember from this unit? Answer the questions using as many vocabulary words as you can without looking in the **Dictionary**. Then compare your list with another student's.

There's a plane ready to take off. Name the parts of the airport and plane that you see below. Then add to your list all the names of the other parts of the airplane and airport building. Include the names of people who work in an airport or travel agency.

blimp

How do you get to school or work? Write all the types of public transportation you know. Then circle the word that describes how you usually travel to school or work.

Do you drive a car? How many parts of a car do you know? List them.

Have you ever seen this sign? Make a list of all the road signs that you see in your neighborhood. If you have room, draw the signs.

B. Notes to Myself

Topic: *My Best Vacation*

Date: _____

What was your best vacation? Where did you go? How did you get there? What did you do? Did you go sight-seeing, touring the countryside, shopping, swimming, or just relaxing? Where did you eat? Write about your *best vacation*. Then share it with someone in your class.

_____

_____

_____

_____

_____

_____

_____

_____

What public transportation do you use to get to school or work? _____.
Draw a map showing how you get from your home to your school or to your workplace. Label the main street and show the side streets. Include the road signs you pass along your route.

Dictionary pages 83–84

A. Look at pages 83 and 84 in the **Dictionary**. Then complete the chart.

	Where Played	Equipment	Players
baseball	baseball park	bat, baseball glove or mitt	pitcher, catcher left fielder
football			
basketball			
tennis			
ice hockey			
soccer			
boxing			
horse racing			

B. Cross out the word or words that don't belong in each sentence. Then rewrite the sentence using words from pages 83 and 84 in the **Dictionary**.

1. ~~Football~~ players sit in a dugout.

    Baseball players sit in a dugout.

2. Baseball players always wear skates.

    _____

3. A jockey always puts a net on the horse.

    _____

4. The fans in the soccer field watch the players run with the football.

    _____

109

C. Circle the letters of the words that complete the relationship.

1.	baseball: park	boxing: **a.** field **b.** court **(c.)** ring **d.** track
2.	umpire: baseball	referee: **a.** horse racing **b.** tennis **c.** volleyball **d.** football
3.	wrestle: mat	horse racing: **a.** ring **b.** track **c.** rink **d.** dugout
4.	bat: ball	hockey stick: **a.** racket **b.** puck **c.** basketball **d.** net
5.	boxing: gloves	baseball: **a.** stick **b.** racket **c.** mask **d.** mitt
6.	football: goal post	ice hockey: **a.** puck **b.** net **c.** home base **d.** mat

D. Write sentences about professional sports using words from Column A, Column B, and Column C.

Column A	Column B	Column C
~~jockey~~	dance	~~saddle~~
goalie	~~sits~~	mask
cheerleaders	uses	racket
tennis player	wears	football
quarterback	plays	stadium

1. *A jockey sits in a saddle.* _____

2. _____

3. _____

4. _____

5. _____

A. Write a letter or letters to describe each sport.

a. uses a ball
b. is usually done outdoors
c. can be dangerous

a, b **1.** golf

_____ **2.** jogging

_____ **3.** weight lifting

_____ **4.** hiking

_____ **5.** cycling

_____ **6.** hunting

_____ **7.** handball

_____ **8.** bowling

_____ **9.** mountain climbing

_____ **10.** croquet

_____ **11.** badminton

_____ **12.** racquetball

B. Look at the pictures on page 85 of the *Dictionary*. Match each item in Column A with a sport in Column B.

Column A

d **1.** backpack

_____ **2.** barbell

_____ **3.** paddle

_____ **4.** alley

_____ **5.** gun

_____ **6.** fairway

_____ **7.** racquet

Column B

a. bowling

b. racquetball

c. golf

d. hiking

e. ping pong

f. weight lifting

g. hunting

C. Which of the sports on page 85 have you tried?

_____

Which one is your favorite? Why?

_____

_____

D. You are beginning a game of golf. Number the following items from 1 to 6 to show the correct order of play.

_____ Hit the ball.

_____ Put your golf ball on the tee.

_____ Hit your ball again.

___1___ Put your tee in the ground.

_____ Choose the right golf club.

_____ Take your golf bag and follow the ball you hit.

E. Rewrite this story. Use fifteen capital letters and ten punctuation marks.

the olympic games

the first recorded olympic competition took place at mount olympus in 776 bc the only event was a race the length of the stadium however additional races and other athletic events were added slowly and the competition was held every four years only greek men who were citizens could enter it was a high honor just to be in the competition the winners received crowns of leaves and they were given many special advantages

_____

_____

_____

_____

_____

_____

A. Circle the word in each row that doesn't belong. Then give a reason.

1. canoeing (swimming) kayaking sailing

   The other sports use boats.
   _____

2. snowmobiling surfing skiing sledding

   _____

3. swimming diving surfing crewing

   _____

4. water skis air tank wet suit mask

   _____

5. sled toboggan ski pole bobsled

   _____

B. José wrote about his vacation in his diary. Complete this diary page using words from page 86 in the *Dictionary*.

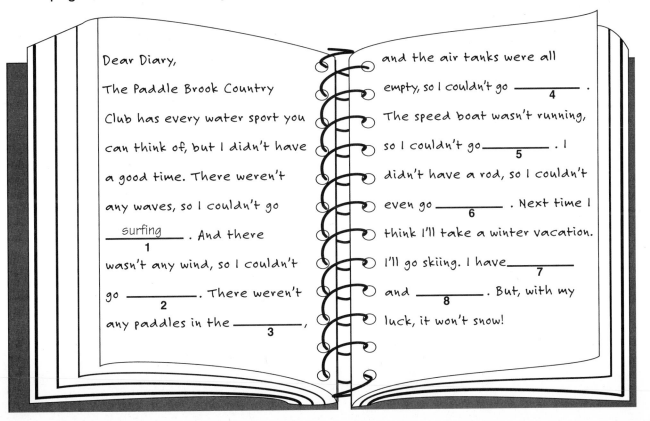

Dear Diary,

The Paddle Brook Country Club has every water sport you can think of, but I didn't have a good time. There weren't any waves, so I couldn't go ___surfing___ . And there
   1
wasn't any wind, so I couldn't go _____ . There weren't
   2
any paddles in the _____ ,
   3

and the air tanks were all empty, so I couldn't go _____ .
   4
The speed boat wasn't running, so I couldn't go_____ . I
   5
didn't have a rod, so I couldn't even go _____ . Next time I
   6
think I'll take a winter vacation. I'll go skiing. I have_____
   7
and _____ . But, with my
   8
luck, it won't snow!

C. Look at the pictures that Mandy took at Camp Apache last summer. Write a story about Mandy's adventures in camp.

My Summer at Camp Apache

I will never forget last summer.

_____

_____

_____

_____

D. Read the questions. Circle the letters of the correct answers.

1. Patrick wants to do a winter sport that will let him sit down most of the time. Which one should he choose?
   a. ice skating
   b. snowmobiling
   c. skiing

2. Luis doesn't like to put his head under water. Which sport should he choose?
   a. snorkeling
   b. scuba diving
   c. canoeing

3. Maria likes to move very, very fast. Which sport would she enjoy most?
   a. sledding
   b. tobogganing
   c. bobsledding

4. After "it" broke, Amelda couldn't move the boat. What broke?
   a. the oar
   b. the tow rope
   c. the water ski

114

A. Look at the pictures below. Write the names of the sports above the pictures. Then write two action words that describe each sport.

1. _____baseball_____

_____slide_____ _____

2. _____

_____ _____

3. _____

_____ _____

4. _____

_____ _____

5. _____

_____ _____

6. _____

_____ _____

B. Complete the conversations using the **-ing** form of the **verbs** in the box.

slide	keep score	bowl
serve	pass	ride

1. **Girl:** Why are you carrying that big, heavy ball?
   Boy: I'm going _____bowling_____.

2. **Girl:** Why did you take a paper and pencil to the ball game?
   Boy: I was _____.

3. **Girl:** He's really throwing that football far!
   Boy: You should say, "He's really _____ that ball far."

4. **Girl:** Look! He's falling down at first base.
   Boy: No, he isn't. He's _____ into the base.

5. **Girl:** Why is she tossing the ball in the air?
   Boy: Because she's _____.

6. **Girl:** Look at the jockey on the horse.
   Boy: I am. He's _____ like a champion.

A. Show where each activity happens. Write **I** if it's only done indoors. Write **O** if it's only done outdoors. Write **B** if it can happen in both places.

_O_ 1. camping

_____ 2. shopping

_____ 3. walking

_____ 4. dancing

_____ 5. going to the movies

_____ 6. taking a vacation

_____ 7. roller skating

_____ 8. exercising

_____ 9. reading

_____ 10. picnicking

_____ 11. going to a museum

_____ 12. going to the beach

B. Answer the questions using the information on the bar graph.

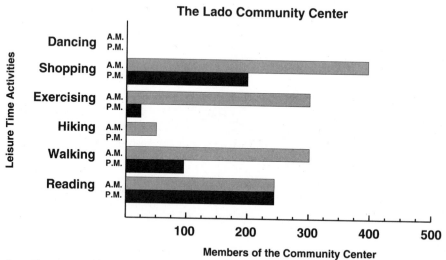

The Lado Community Center

1. Are the members of the Community Center more active during the day or the evening? _____the day_____

2. How many members are in the Community Center? _____

3. What is the most popular leisure time activity? _____

4. What activity isn't preferred at night? _____

5. Do people exercise more in the morning or in the evening? _____

6. Three hundred members of The Lado Community Center enjoy _____ and _____.

7. What activity is enjoyed as much at night as during the day?

_____

8. Would people rather read or shop at night ? _____

Add this information to the graph.

1. Show that 75 people go dancing during the day.

2. Show that 350 members of the community go dancing at night.

A. How is each pair of pictures different? Study each pair and write a sentence explaining at least one difference.

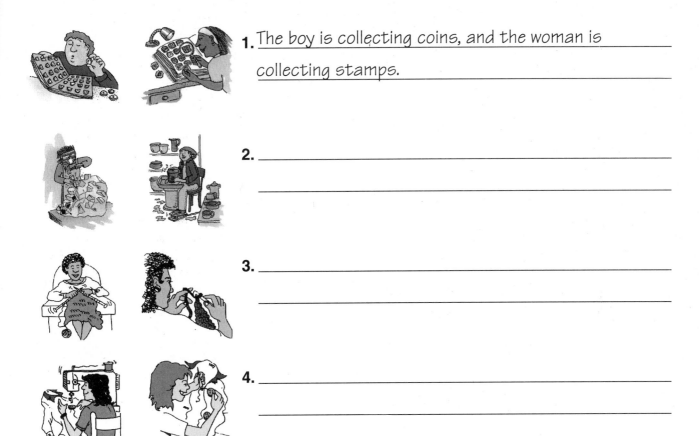

1. The boy is collecting coins, and the woman is collecting stamps.

2. _____

3. _____

4. _____

B. Match each item in Column A with a hobby in Column B.

Column A

d **1.** yarn

____ **2.** clay

____ **3.** hoop

____ **4.** fabric

____ **5.** hook

____ **6.** album

Column B

a. pottery

b. stamp collecting

c. crocheting

d. knitting

e. sewing

f. embroidery

A. Cross out the item that doesn't belong in each sentence. Then write a word from page 90 in the **Dictionary** to make the sentence correct.

1. Use ~~inks~~ with a stereo system.   headphones

2. Speakers are part of cameras.   _____

3. Televisions are used to play compact disks.   _____

4. Movie projectors play video cassettes.   _____

5. VCR means video cassette record.   _____

6. Receivers are parts of video cameras.   _____

7. Sound comes out of movie projectors.   _____

8. There are volume controls on cameras.   _____

9. Slides are larger than compact disks.   _____

10. Film is developed into prints and cassettes.   _____

B. Look at page 90 in the **Dictionary**. Write the names of the electronic and photographic equipment that is on sale. Complete the chart with two more ads.

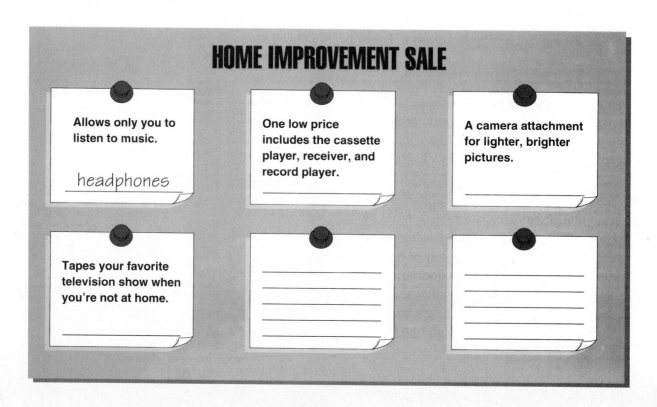

HOME IMPROVEMENT SALE

Allows only you to listen to music.

headphones

One low price includes the cassette player, receiver, and record player.

A camera attachment for lighter, brighter pictures.

Tapes your favorite television show when you're not at home.

A. Look at page 91 in the **Dictionary**. Then complete the story using prepositions from the box.

near	with	on	at	across

Bill and Tina's Party

Everyone is having a wonderful time ____*at*____ the party. Bill and Tina are
₁

talking _____ some of their guests, while the other guests are standing
₂

_____ the refreshment table. The disc jockey is putting records
₃

_____ the turntable, and a few guests are dancing _____ him. A
₄ ₅

young boy is reaching _____ the table to move a piece on the game table,
₆

while a man is standing _____ the table watching him. Friends are laughing
₇

_____ old friends, and some guests are making new friends _____
₈ ₉

the party. Bill and Tina can see their guests dancing and eating _____ the
₁₀

room. They know everyone is having a wonderful time!

B. Complete the conversations using the correct forms of the verbs in the box.

laugh		shake hands		introduce		eat
	dance		invite		play	

1. **Boy:** Natalia didn't come to the party.
   Girl: Maybe she wasn't ____*invited*____ .

2. **Boy:** Look, Kim Soo is _____ her friend Sam to John.
   Girl: Is that why they're _____ ?

3. **Boy:** Aren't you hungry? You haven't _____ all night.
   Girl: I _____ before I came to the party.

4. **Boy:** Alex has never met Bill before.
   Girl: So, let's _____ them.

5. **Boy:** The guests are tired. They've been _____ to the fast music all night.
   Girl: Ask them to _____ some games.

6. **Boy:** The host just told a very funny story.
   Girl: So that's why all the guests are _____ .

A. Look at page 92 in the **Dictionary**. Rewrite the sentences using the contractions in the box.

they're	he's	she's	it's

1. *The audience* is having a wonderful time.

   They're having a wonderful time.

2. When *the curtain* is closed, the show is over.

   _____

3. *The actor* is performing his last show of the year.

   _____

4. *The ballerina* is dancing with the ballet dancer.

   _____

5. *The lead singers* in the rock band are singing very loud.

   _____

6. *The people* in the balcony are enjoying the show.

   _____

B. Alphabetize the words in the box. Write the number of syllables in each word.

theater	actress	tutu	ballerina	scenery
actor	spotlight	baton	curtain	conductor

1. _____actor_____ [2]   6. _____ [   ]

2. _____ [   ]   7. _____ [   ]

3. _____ [   ]   8. _____ [   ]

4. _____ [   ]   9. _____ [   ]

5. _____ [   ]   10. _____ [   ]

C. Complete the crossword puzzle using the performing arts words from page 92 in the *Dictionary*.

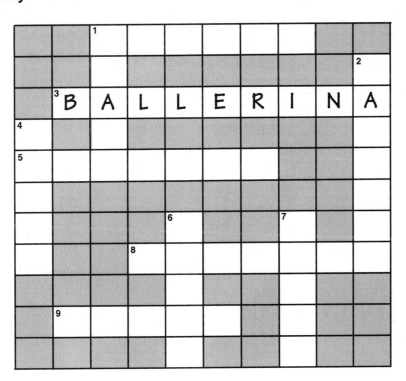

Across

1. A band listens to the lead _____ to keep the beat.

3. Toe shoes and a tutu are worn by a _ballerina_ .

5. The people in the _____ are very noisy before the rock concert starts.

8. The _____ is the background on a stage.

9. A _____ is a stick used by a conductor to lead a band.

Down

1. Actors perform on a _____ .

2. The _____ is the upper area of seats in a theater.

4. The music _____ holds the sheet music for the musicians.

6. A person who performs on stage is an _____ .

7. The audience sits in their _____ as they watch a show.

A. Choose the best ending for each sentence.

1. The musician
   a. played the ukelele with a bow.
   b. thought the piccolo was very heavy.
   (c.) banged the cymbals together.

2. An organ
   a. is a brass instrument.
   b. has black and white keys.
   c. looks like a harmonica.

3. The tuba
   a. is made of wood.
   b. has four strings.
   c. is larger than a French horn.

4. The cello
   a. looks a lot like a bass.
   b. is a woodwind instrument.
   c. is never played with a bow.

5. The harmonica
   a. is played with two hands.
   b. sounds like a tambourine.
   c. is a wind instrument.

6. The violinist
   a. uses drumsticks.
   b. needs a baton.
   c. needs a bow.

B. Answer these questions using one or more words from page 93 in the *Dictionary*.

1. Which instruments might be easy to play?

   drum, tambourine, harmonica

2. Which instruments do you usually find in a church?

3. Samir wants to sing and play at the same time. What instruments could he choose to play?

4. What are the three heaviest instruments?

5. Which instrument(s) have you played?

A. **Vocabulary Practice**

How many words do you remember from this unit? Answer the questions using as many vocabulary words as you can without looking in the *Dictionary*. Then compare your list with another student's.

List the sports or activities you see below. What equipment is used in these activities? List them. Then list other sports, activities, and hobbies that aren't shown and name the equipment they use.

Sport	Equipment
golf	club, ball, tee

What are the guests doing?

laughing

Make a list of musical instruments. What instrument do you play? Circle the instrument you play or would like to play.

violin

B.

NoTes

Topic: *My Leisure Time*

Date: _____

What do you do when you're not working or in school? Do you play an instrument? Do you enjoy playing or watching a sport? Use the words in this unit to tell about your hobbies and how you spend your *leisure time.*

_____

_____

_____

_____

_____

_____

_____

Tell about your experience with one of the following:

1. A recent vacation

2. Summer camp

3. A sporting event

4. A birthday, anniversary, or holiday party

5. Your performance or experience at a symphony, concert, or play

_____

_____

_____

_____

_____

_____

_____

80. WEDDING   *Dictionary page 94*

A. Read the story. Underline all the vocabulary words from page 94 in the **Dictionary.**

A Wedding

A wedding is a very happy occasion. In the United States the celebration starts with an engagement ring and ends with a marriage license. On the wedding day, the groom arrives with the best man. The best man is often the groom's brother or his best friend. His job is to be sure the groom doesn't forget anything. The groom and the best man are usually dressed in tuxedos. Each one has a boutonniere on his collar. The justice of the peace or religious leader arrives early.

A little later, the bride arrives. She usually wears a long, white wedding dress with a soft veil over her face. She carries a bouquet of her favorite flowers. Her maid of honor and her bridesmaids help her get ready. Sometimes the couple ask young children from their families to join in the ceremony. They may choose a little boy to be the ring bearer and a little girl to be the flower girl.

After the wedding, there is often a reception where the guests can eat and dance and talk with the bride and groom. As the celebration comes to an end, the bride and groom cut the wedding cake and give each guest a piece. Some people take this cake home.

B. Write sentences using items from Column A and Column B.

Column A	Column B
~~maid of honor~~	tuxedos
wedding reception	little boy
groom and best man	~~the bride~~
bride and groom	after the wedding
ring bearer	head table

1. _The maid of honor helps the bride prepare for her wedding._

2. _____

3. _____

4. _____

5. _____

A. Answer the following questions. Then share your answers with a friend.

Birthday Questionnaire

How many birthday cards do you send every year? _____

How many birthday cards do you get? _____

When was the last time you had a party for your birthday? _____

Who planned the party? _____

How many guests were there? _____

Where did the party take place? _____

What refreshments were served? _____

Did you get any gifts? _____

If so, what did you get? _____

Did you have a birthday cake? _____

What did it look like? _____

Did you blow out the candles? _____

If so, what did you wish for? _____

B. Write the following words in alphabetical order.

candles	refreshments	balloon	magician
birthday	present	guests	rabbit

1. _balloon_

2. _____

3. _____

4. _____

5. _____

6. _____

7. _____

8. _____

A. Look at the pictures on page 96 in the **Dictionary.**

1. What's hanging from the Christmas tree?
   ornament _____ _____

2. What decorations are near the fireplace?
   _____ _____ _____

3. What's under the Christmas tree? _____

4. Who's outside the window? _____

5. What's in the basket on the floor? _____

6. Who's the man with the white beard? _____

7. What's in the sleigh? _____

8. What are the reindeer doing? _____

B. Word search: Find seventeen words that remind you of the Christmas holiday. Circle them.

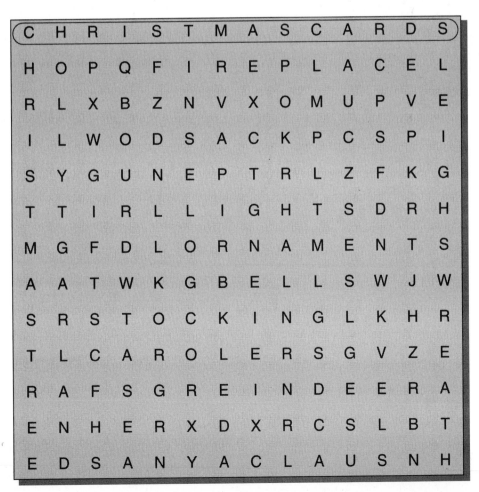

C	H	R	I	S	T	M	A	S	C	A	R	D	S
H	O	P	Q	F	I	R	E	P	L	A	C	E	L
R	L	X	B	Z	N	V	X	O	M	U	P	V	E
I	L	W	O	D	S	A	C	K	P	C	S	P	I
S	Y	G	U	N	E	P	T	R	L	Z	F	K	G
T	T	I	R	L	L	I	G	H	T	S	D	R	H
M	G	F	D	L	O	R	N	A	M	E	N	T	S
A	A	T	W	K	G	B	E	L	L	S	W	J	W
S	R	S	T	O	C	K	I	N	G	L	K	H	R
T	L	C	A	R	O	L	E	R	S	G	V	Z	E
R	A	F	S	G	R	E	I	N	D	E	E	R	A
E	N	H	E	R	X	D	X	R	C	S	L	B	T
E	D	S	A	N	Y	A	C	L	A	U	S	N	H

C. Complete the sentences using words from page 97 in the *Dictionary.*

1. The guests at the New Ⓨ E A R 'S Eve party get noisier as midnight approaches.

2. When the clock strikes midnight __ __ Ⓞ __ __ __ __ __ is thrown in the air.

3. A __ __ Ⓞ __ __ is made with two glasses of champagne.

4. __ __ __ Ⓞ Ⓞ __ __ __ __ light up the sky with a lot of noise.

5. Almost everyone wears a Ⓞ __ __ __ Ⓞ Ⓞ __ __ on New Year's Eve.

6. The __ Ⓞ Ⓞ __ __ __ is an important animal in the Chinese New Year celebration.

7. __ __ __ Ⓞ __ __ __ __ __ are long, thin pieces of paper.

8. Many people drink __ __ __ __ Ⓞ __ __ __ __ on New Year's Eve.

Rearrange the letters in the circles to answer the following question.

What do you say to a friend, at the stroke of midnight, on New Year's Eve?

__ __ __ __ __   __ __ __   __ __ __ __

D. Kim is writing a note to her friend. She is telling her about a special new year's celebration. Complete the letter using words from page 97 in the *Dictionary*.

Dear Laura,

I just spent New Year's Eve with some Chinese friends. No one wore

party hats , and nobody threw _____ They didn't even drink
    1   2

_____ There was plenty of noise, but it didn't come from
    3

_____. It came from drums and _____. The party wasn't at
    4   5

someone's house. They had a _____ through the streets, and some
                                    6

_____ carried a _____ saying "Happy New Year" in Chinese.
    7   8

At the head of the parade was a big _____. It was my best New
                                      9

Year's celebration ever! Wish you were here!

Love,

Kim

128

E. Write the names of the Halloween costumes in alphabetic order.

witch	ghost	black cat	princess	clown
skeleton	pirate	mummy	devil	bat

1. _bat_

2. _____

3. _____

4. _____

5. _____

6. _____

7. _____

8. _____

9. _____

10. _____

F. How are these two pictures different? Study them and write four sentences telling about the differences.

A   B

1. _There's a clown in Picture A and a witch in Picture B._____.

2. _____

3. _____

4. _____

129

G. Cross out the word or words that don't belong in each sentence. Then rewrite the sentences using words from page 99 in the *Dictionary.*

1. I'd like some ~~stuffing~~ to drink.

   I'd like some apple cider to drink.

2. The Mayflower is my favorite part of the Thanksgiving meal.

   _____

3. Please give me a pilgrim so I can cut the turkey.

   _____

4. That turkey is full of pumpkin pie.

   _____

5. The Pilgrims sat down with the turkeys for the first Thanksgiving.

   _____

6. The Mayflower brought the Native Americans to America.

   _____

H. Find words from this unit on **Celebrations and Holidays** that rhyme with the following words. Write the words below.

1. host _____ghost_____   4. play _____   7. sleeve _____

2. back _____   5. sock _____   8. trail _____

3. broom _____   6. handle _____   9. shower _____

I. Talk to a few friends in your class. Ask them about their favorite holidays. Complete the chart.

Name	Favorite holiday	Holiday food	Holiday activity	Why do you like this holiday?
[your name]				
[friend]				

A. **Vocabulary Practice**

How many words do you remember from this unit? Complete the chart using as many vocabulary words as you can without looking in the *Dictionary*. Then compare your list with another student's.

Name *all* the holidays and occasions you celebrate. On the chart below write all the vocabulary words that remind you of these events.

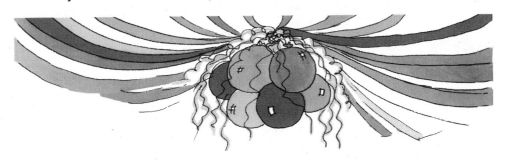

Holidays	activities	foods	clothing	decorations
Christmas	wrapping presents	ham	bells on coats	tinsel
Other occasions				

B. **Notes to Myself**

NoTes

Topic: *My Favorite Holiday*

Date: _____

Is there one holiday that is more *special to you* than any of the other holidays? Is this holiday an American holiday or a holiday that is celebrated in your native country? Use words from this unit to help you write about your favorite holiday and why it is so *special to you.*

_____

_____

_____

_____

_____

_____

_____

Topic: *A Recent Celebration*

Have you recently been to an engagement party, bridal shower, wedding, anniversary party, birthday party for a baby or a grandparent, or graduation party? Have you just celebrated someone's job promotion? Write about a special occasion that you have celebrated with a friend or with your family.

_____

_____

_____

_____

_____

_____

84. **THE UNIVERSE**   *Dictionary pages 100–101*

A.   Look at pages 100 and 101 in the **Dictionary.** List the nine planets. Begin with the one closest to the sun.

   1. ___Mercury___   4. _____   7. _____

   2. _____   5. _____   8. _____

   3. _____   6. _____   9. _____

B.   Study the picture of the Universe. Then match each item in Column A with an item in Column B.

   Column A   **Column B**

   _d_ 1. comet   **a.** the smallest planet

   ____ 2. meteor   **b.** how the earth moves around the sun

   ____ 3. Little Dipper   **c.** shooting star

   ____ 4. Saturn   **d.** tail

   ____ 5. Pluto   **e.** the largest planet

   ____ 6. Jupiter   **f.** near the North Star

   ____ 7. orbit   **g.** rings

C.   Use complete sentences to answer these questions about the Universe.

   1. Which is larger, the sun or Jupiter?
       The sun is larger than Jupiter.

   2. What part of the Universe, besides Earth, have men walked on?

       _____

   3. Which planet is called "the red planet"?

       _____

   4. What is a constellation?

       _____

133

A. Choose the best ending for each sentence. Circle **a**, **b**, or **c**.

1. Islands
   a. are never found in lakes.
   (b.) have water on all sides.
   c. are always near mountains.

2. A beach
   a. is usually found on a mountain.
   b. is part of a valley.
   c. always has water near it.

3. A river
   a. is never found in a valley.
   b. is the same as a beach.
   c. leads to a bay or a wider body of water.

4. There is no such thing as
   a. a tiny mountain.
   b. a flat plain.
   c. a big ocean.

B. Follow these instructions.

1. Draw a circle. Label it Earth.
2. Draw some latitude lines. Label them.
3. Draw some longitude lines. Label them.
4. Label the North Pole and the South Pole.
5. Label the Equator.
6. Draw the continent you came from. Write its name.

A. Read the questions. Then circle the letters of the correct answers.

1. Hector wants to take a vacation where the weather is usually warm and there are lots of beaches. Where should he go?
   a. Vermont
   (b.) Florida
   c. Kansas

2. Phong wants to see how people live in the middle of the United States. Which state might he visit?
   a. California
   b. Kansas
   c. Maine

3. Maria lives in New York City. Her son has a job in the state farthest from that city. Where does he work?
   a. Colorado
   b. Texas
   c. California

4. What is the smallest state in the United States?
   a. Delaware
   b. Connecticut
   c. Rhode Island

B. Do you live in the United States?

If you do . . . (Answer these questions)	If you don't . . . (Answer these questions)
1. What state do you live in?	1. What state would you like to visit?
2. What are the two biggest cities?	Why?
3. What is the capital?	2. What would you like to do and see there?
4. What other state would you like to visit?	3. Where do you live now?
Why?	

C. Complete the crossword puzzle using the names of the states in the United States.

| ¹M | I | ²S | S | ³I | S | ⁴S | I | P | P | I |

(crossword grid with numbered cells: 5, 6, 7, 8, 9, 10, 11)

Across
This state:

1. is also the name of the longest river in the United States.
5. is east of Nevada and west of Colorado.
7. is between Georgia and Mississippi.
8. is south of Minnesota and north of Missouri.
9. is the largest state in the U.S.
10. is in the northeast corner of the U.S.
11. is the most northwestern state in the U.S.

Down
This state:

1. has a name that comes from the Spanish word for "mountain." It's next to Idaho.
2. is northeast of Georgia. (two words)
3. is named for the Indians who lived there. It's south of Michigan.
4. is south of North Dakota. (two words)
6. is a group of islands southwest of the mainland of the U.S.

A. Look at the map on page 106 of the **Dictionary.** Write **T** for True or **F** for False.

___T___ **1.** Brazil is the largest country in South America.

_____ **2.** Chile is a long, narrow country.

_____ **3.** Haiti and the Dominican Republic are on the same island.

_____ **4.** Mexico touches the U.S. and Nicaragua.

_____ **5.** Cuba is larger than Puerto Rico.

_____ **6.** Costa Rica is in Central America.

_____ **7.** Guyana is an island.

_____ **8.** Guatemala is in Central America.

_____ **9.** Panama is between Colombia and Costa Rica.

_____ **10.** Canada is larger than Mexico.

B. Look at the map on page 106 in the **Dictionary.** Write a letter or letters to help identify the country.

a. borders on an ocean
b. is an island
c. is in South America
d. is in Central America

___a, c___ **1.** Argentina   _____ **7.** El Salvador

_____ **2.** Canada   _____ **8.** Ecuador

_____ **3.** Bolivia   _____ **9.** Puerto Rico

_____ **4.** Honduras   _____ **10.** Mexico

_____ **5.** Paraguay   _____ **11.** Peru

_____ **6.** Uruguay   _____ **12.** Cuba

C. Choose one country from the map on page 106. List some facts about it.

_____

_____

_____

_____

A. Study the map of Europe on page 107 in the **Dictionary** for a few minutes. Then close the **Dictionary** and complete the map with the names of the countries that you remember. Add the names of other countries that you know.

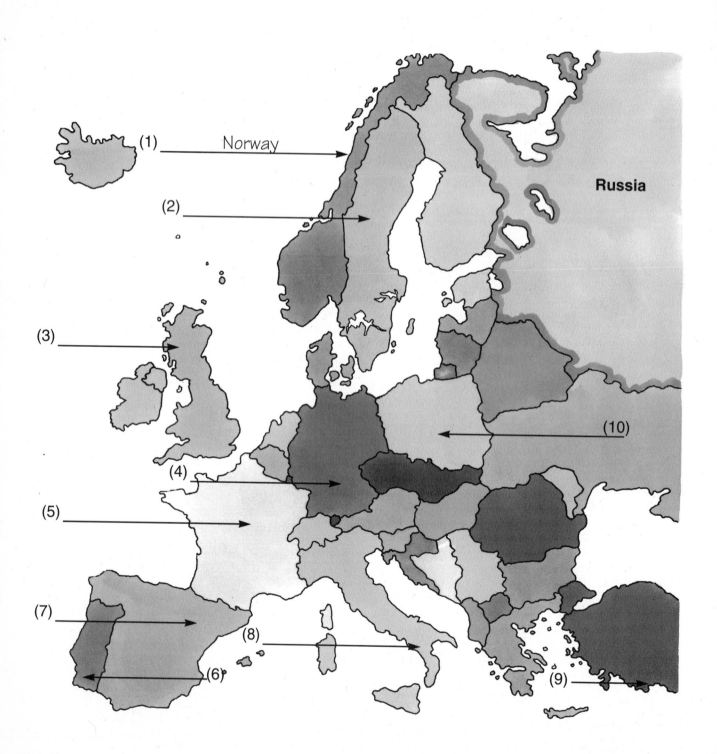

(1) _____ Norway

(2) _____

Russia

(3) _____

(4) _____

(5) _____

(7) _____

(8) _____

(6) _____

(9) _____

(10) _____

A. Study the map of Africa on page 108 in the **Dictionary.** Then answer the following questions.

1. Name three countries in the northern part of Africa.

   _____Morocco_____   _____   _____

2. Name three countries in central Africa.

   _____   _____   _____

3. Name three countries in the southern part of Africa.

   _____   _____   _____

4. Name three island countries.

   _____   _____   _____

5. Name three countries that do not touch an ocean.

   _____   _____   _____

B. Write *near* or *far away from.*

1. Algeria is _far away from_ Mozambique.
2. The Congo is _____ Sudan.
3. South Africa is _____ Angola.
4. Libya is _____ Egypt.
5. Ghana is _____ Nigeria.
6. Niger is _____ Tanzania.

C. Write *north, south, east,* or *west.*

1. Libya is _north_ of South Africa.
2. The Ivory Coast is _____ of Sudan.
3. Somalia is _____ of Guinea.
4. Tunisia is _____ of Angola.
5. Zaire is _____ of Chad.
6. Nigeria is _____ of Liberia.

D. Choose one country in Africa and tell some things you know about it.

_____

_____

_____

_____

A. Look at page 109 in the **Dictionary.** Then write the names of these countries in order of their size. Start with the largest.

| Turkey |
| China |
| Australia |
| Lebanon |
| India |
| Saudi Arabia |

1. _____

2. _____

3. _____

4. _____

5. _____

6. _____

B. Complete part of the map of Asia by drawing and labeling the following countries: Iran, Afghanistan, Pakistan, India, Nepal, Bhutan, Bangladesh, and Burma.

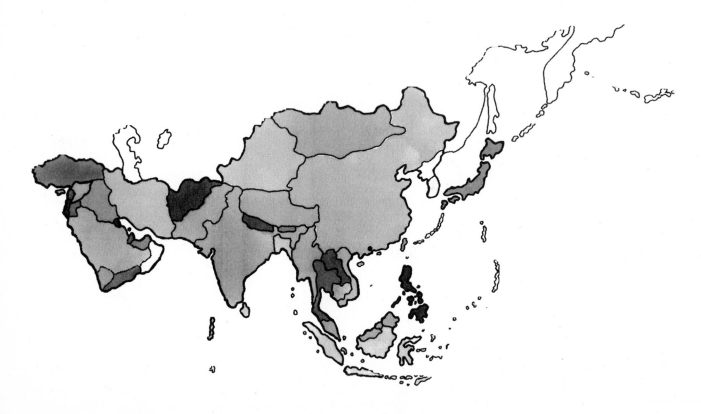

A. Study the world map on pages 110 and 111 in the **Dictionary.** Then complete the chart. (You may need other maps to help you.)

	Mountain Ranges	Deserts	Rivers and Lakes	Oceans and Seas
Africa	Atlas			
North America			Great Lakes	
Asia				Sea of Japan
South America		Andes		
Europe				Arctic Ocean

B. Look at the world map and the above chart. What have you learned about the continents in the world? Write some of your own conclusions.

1. _____ There aren't any major deserts in North America. _____

2. _____

3. _____

4. _____

5. _____

C. Answer these questions about your native country. You can use information that is not on the map of the world.

My Country: _____
1. What continent is it on? _____
2. Does an ocean touch it? _____
If so, what ocean? _____
3. Are there mountains in your country? _____
If so, which ones? _____
4. Are there deserts? _____
If so, which ones? _____
5. What lakes or gulfs are there? _____
6. What rivers are there? _____
7. What is the most beautiful part of your native country? _____

D. Word Search: Find the names of the seven continents and five oceans. Circle them.

```
A  T  L  A  N  T  I  C  X  A  J  U
S  R  I  N  D  I  A  N  O  S  P  E
N  O  R  T  H  A  M  E  R  I  C  A
J  E  P  A  C  I  F  I  C  A  K  M
W  U  F  R  G  N  U  B  A  O  Z  Q
A  R  M  C  X  B  D  G  F  P  I  H
S  O  U  T  H  A  M  E  R  I  C  A
T  P  N  I  P  L  S  H  I  T  V  R
G  E  L  C  F  G  Y  P  C  Z  O  W
O  X  R  A  U  S  T  R  A  L  I  A
```

E. Write the names of the continents that touch each ocean.

Atlantic North America, South America

Arctic _____

Pacific _____

Antarctic _____

Indian _____

A. **Vocabulary Practice**

How many words do you remember from this unit? Answer the questions using as many vocabulary words as you can without looking in the **Dictionary**. Then compare your answers with another student's.

Look at this world map. Find the continents. Label them. What continent is your native country in? Circle it. Put an **X** on the continent where you are now. Then find the major oceans and label them. (Antarctica and the Antarctic Ocean aren't on this map.)

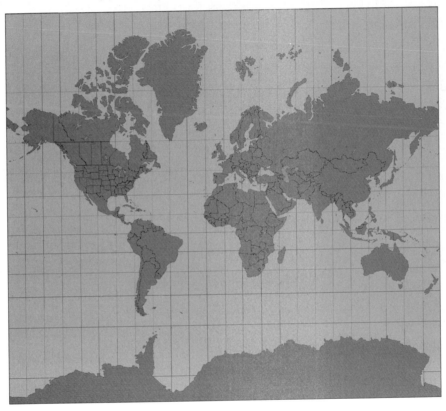

How many planets do you recognize? Label them.

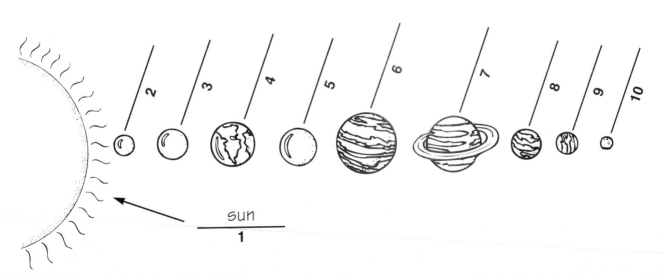

B. Notes to Myself

NoTes

Topic: *My vacation*

Date: _____

Have you been away recently? Were you out of the country or visiting local areas? Were you touring, sightseeing, camping, skiing, or visiting friends or relatives? Write and address a postcard to a friend or relative from your vacation spot. Describe the weather and your overall impression of the trip.

Take that dream vacation you've always wanted. Pack your bags. You're off to _____. Write about why you chose that dream vacation spot and what you hope to see when you get there.

_____

_____

_____

_____

_____

_____

_____

93.   MEASURES

Dictionary page 112

A.   Study the words on page 112 of the **Dictionary** that show size, weight, length, width, and speed. Then choose two or three of these words to describe each item below.

1.

a.   ___big, long, heavy___

b.   ___small___

2.

a.   _____

b.   _____

3.

a.   _____

b.   _____

4.

a.   _____

b.   _____

B.   Look at the musical instruments on page 93 of the **Dictionary.** Complete the sentences using the words in the box. Some words can be used more than once.

big	bigger	biggest	small	smaller	smallest
short	shorter	shortest	tall	taller	tallest

1.   A recorder is _____smaller_____ than a flute.

2.   A piccolo is the _____ of all the woodwinds.

3.   A harp is _____ than a piano.

4.   A cello is _____ than a violin, but the bass is the _____ of all.

5.   An organ is _____ than a piano.

6.   The harmonica is the _____ instrument of all.

7.   A tambourine is _____ than cymbals.

8.   A drumstick is _____ than a bow.

C. Complete the conversations using the measurements in the box.

Measurements		
2 cups	=	1 pint
2 pints	=	1 quart
4 quarts	=	1 gallon

1. **Bob:** I'm so hungry I could eat 4 cups of ice cream.
   Sally: I suggest you buy __2__ pints.

2. **Tom:** Dad wants me to get *4 pints* of oil for his truck.
   Mary: Then ask the mechanic for _____ *quarts*.

3. **Jim:** My room needs painting. I bet I'll need at least *8 quarts* of paint to cover my whole room.
   Ted: Buy at least _____ *gallons*.

4. **Kim:** Mom told me she's baking a few of her favorite cakes tonight. She said she'll need *5 cups* of milk.
   Paul: Let's buy her _____ *quarts* to make sure she has enough.

5. **Lisa:** If Bill and Tom are coming for the weekend, we'll need a lot of orange juice. Let's buy *3 pints.*
   Tina: It's probably cheaper to buy _____ *quarts.*

6. **Tom:** My sister says she *loves* yogurt. She could eat *a whole gallon* of it!
   Susan: That means she could eat ____ *cups—one at a time!*

D. Write sentences using words from Column A, Column B, and Column C. Use the -er form of the **adjectives** in Column B.

Column A	Column B	Column C
~~cup~~	light	lake
ocean	~~small~~	sidewalk
road	tall	~~gallon~~
car	deep	bicycle
man	wide	baby
feather	fast	book

1. A cup is smaller than a gallon.

2. _____

3. _____

4. _____

5. _____

6. _____

146

A. Look at the page in the **Dictionary** and read the sentence. Write the season.

1. *Page 98* The children are bobbing for apples. _____fall_____

2. *Page 86* There are three children on the toboggan. _____

3. *Page 66* There are apples on the tree. _____

4. *Page 73* There are acorns on the oak tree. _____

5. *Page 99* They're having Thanksgiving dinner. _____

6. *Page 24* There are vegetables in the garden. _____

7. *Page 96* Santa Claus is coming. _____

8. *Page 53* The students are graduating from college. _____

B. Complete the conversations using the weather words from page 113 in the **Dictionary.**

1. **Paul:** Why is everyone covering their windows with wood?
   Wanda: They heard there's a _____ coming this way.

2. **Steve:** Did you hear that crash of thunder?
   Paula: Yes, and I saw the _____ , too.

3. **Carlos:** I want to go skiing tomorrow.
   Cristina: Then I hope we have a lot of _____ tonight.

4. **Stan:** I just lost my hat!
   Maria: That's what happens when we have _____ weather.

5. **Roberto:** Will you go to the beach this afternoon?
   Kelly: Probably not. It looks kind of _____ .

6. **Adam:** Is that rain? It sure is making a lot of noise on the window.
   Nancy: No, it's _____ .

A. Talk to some students in your class. Complete the chart.

Student A: What day is it? _____

Student B: It's _____.

Student A: What's today's date? _____

Student B: Today is _____.

Student	Birthday	Age	Number of people in family	Name, day, and date of favorite holiday this year

B. Write the following math problems in words.

1. $5 + 7 = 12$

Five plus seven equals twelve. _____

2. $13 + 7 = 20$

_____

3. $90 - 50 = 40$

_____ minus _____

4. $10 \times 100 = 1000$

_____ times _____

5. $90 \times 100 = 900$

_____

A. Look at the supermarket on pages 44 and 45 in the Dictionary. Complete the story using the prepositions in the box.

through	above	in	on
near	around	inside	
in front of	one	below	far from

Supermarket Shopping

There is a lot of activity in the supermarket on pages 44 and 45 in the **Dictionary!**

One customer has fruits and vegetables _____in_____ his shopping basket. He is

1

talking to the manager, who is walking _____ the store. Another customer is

2

buying meat. Others are busy looking _____ the store for different grocery

3

items that are _____ their grocery lists.

4

This supermarket has many different departments. Each item is found

_____ a different location. Eggs are _____ the cheese

5 6

_____ the dairy department. Cans of fruits and vegetables are

7

_____ the shelves _____ the baby foods. Fresh fruits and

8 9

vegetable are _____ each other and can be weighed _____ the

10 11

scale. The video center is _____ the meat department, but it's only a short

12

walk _____ the store to find it.

13

Right now, the cashier is standing _____ the cash register, giving a

14

receipt to a customer. The customer's groceries are _____ the shopping bag

15

_____ the conveyor belt. The customer doesn't live _____ the

16 17

supermarket. She'll be home soon, to enjoy the rest of her day.

B. Look at the supermarket picture on pages 44 and 45. Write **T** for True or **F** for False.

_F___ **1.** The stock clerk is *near* the baker.

_____ **2.** There is a man *behind* the deli counter.

_____ **3.** The baby foods are *below* the canned fruits.

_____ **4.** The produce section is *far from* the video center.

_____ **5.** The eggs are *above* the cheese.

_____ **6.** The meat section is *across from* the health aids.

_____ **7.** The dairy products are *beside* the fish.

_____ **8.** The manager is standing *at* the cash register.

_____ **9.** A customer is standing *in front of* the meats.

_____ **10.** The produce section is just *beyond* the beverages.

C. A dog was following Andrea's cat. Draw a line to show where they ran.

They ran

1. in front of the rock

2. under the fence.

3. around the tree.

4. over the bench.

5. through the bushes, and

6. into the house.

X
Start
here

A. **Vocabulary Practice**

How many words do you remember from this unit? Answer the questions using as many vocabulary words as you can without looking in the **Dictionary**. Then compare your answers with another student's.

Where is the detective?

at (the door)
_____
_____
_____

Where is the thief going?

_____
_____
_____
_____

What season is it?

_____

Describe today's weather.

_____
_____
_____
_____

Read the days of the week and the months of the year on the calendars below.

Close your eyes and repeat them. Then write them in order. Check your spelling.

B.

Topic: *My Schedule*

Date: _____

What month is it? Complete the calendar for the current month, including the days and dates. Then insert your schedule. Include tests and deadlines for homework assignments, doctor appointments, birthdays and other occasions and celebrations, holidays, and social plans.

This month is _____

SUNDAY	MONDAY	TUESDAY	WEDNESDAY	THURSDAY	FRIDAY	SATURDAY
				1	2	3
4	5	6	7	8	9	10
11	12	13	14	15	16	17
18	19	20	21	22	23	24
25	26	27	28	29	30	31

Some personal questions:

Is this a busy month for you? _____

What don't you *have time* to do this month? What will have to wait until next month?

_____

What did you *want* to do this month that you won't have time to do?

_____

What's your favorite month? Why?   _____

_____

_____